WINNING WORDS
Prizewinners in the Faber and Faber
Write-A-Story Competition

To coincide with the launch of the children's paperback list in 1989, Faber and Faber launched a children's Write-A-Story competition, asking readers of up to twelve years of age to send us a story of no more than 1,500 words, to be judged by the Poet Laureate Ted Hughes.

With over 2,000 entries of an extraordinarily high standard, the judging was long and hard, but in this delightfully illustrated volume appear the winning stories, celebrating the imagination and skill of just some of the authors of the future.

With a Foreword by Ted Hughes, this is an anthology to enchant children and adults alike – and to encourage young writers everywhere.

WINNING WORDS

Prizewinners
in the Faber and Faber
Write-A-Story
Competition

Chosen and with a Foreword by
Ted Hughes

Illustrated by Genevieve Webster
after ideas by the authors

faber and faber

LONDON · BOSTON

First published in 1991
by Faber and Faber Limited
3 Queen Square London WC1N 3AU

Photoset by Parker Typesetting Service Leicester
Printed in Great Britain by
Cox and Wyman Ltd, Reading, Berkshire

A CIP record for this book
is available from the British Library

ISBN 0 571 16156 1

Contents

Publisher's note

The last three stories were the winning entries in a separate Write-A-Story Competition open to young writers of all races in South Africa and Namibia. The upper age limit was sixteen and the judges were led by Eve Jammy of Young Reading, Johannesburg, in cooperation with Faber and Faber Limited and Penguin South Africa. Faber and Faber wish to thank Eve Jammy and Penguin South Africa for their involvement in this venture, and especially all the young writers who entered the competition.

Foreword

It was not a simple job, picking out these stories from a high pile. But I had a simple rule. I chose the ones that seemed to me to have given their authors most enjoyment. The whirl of action around the surprising two-petalled flower in 'Firfrizzle and the Cater-dragon' must have been great fun to write. I wonder if the shadow-nicker alarmed its author as much as it alarmed me. All these writers gave themselves a thrill or a laugh. They climb into spaceships, or grapple with robots, or fly off into the brains of computers or into future time, with the greatest zest. Or they meet the Swamp Child, or the escaped lion. Or they become an ant, a python, and look back at the human world with weird eyes. If they stick to the local park, it's as a lost explorer, a scientist coming out of his laboratory shaken and wiser. Even the four-year-old sleeper sends his wart to the top of Pendle Hill, where the witches danced.

Some of these mind-games are complicated and skilful. Some are simple and artful. But all solve problems, greater or smaller. And all are worth playing. I am sure readers will enjoy playing them over again, as much as I have.

Ted Hughes

Mechanical Superhero?

Haggai Scolnicov

On 17 June 2157 the NDP robot series was taken out of circulation, compensation being promised by the manufacturers to the owners.

Alexander Neville, robot designer, sighed and leaned back in his armchair. Programming robots was not an easy job. The implementation of various operating techniques in electronic circuits demanded great skill and concentration. Small red and blue lights blinked annoyingly at him as he tried to program a cleaning robot; apparently, using a mop was not all that simple. The computer set into his desk aggravated him further by announcing: INSUFFICIENT COORDINATES. ROBOT WILL ENTER ERROR CONDITION 73. That meant he'd have to try again. Never before had he considered the complex mathematical equations involved in mopping up floors.

At that point he heard a timid knock. 'Come in!' he called. The door to his study opened and a small robot rolled in, turning slowly towards Alexander. Its gleaming titanium-alloy body was cylindrical in shape. It was about 1 metre high and 30 centimetres in diameter. A metallic dome on its top served as a head, bearing various electronic sensors and the speech apparatus. Some arms (eight at the most)

3

hung limply by its body, lifeless until activated. Last but not least, an assortment of wheels and leg-like constructions could just be glimpsed beneath the main structure; they were suited to most types of terrain, both natural and man-made.

'Hello, Endeepee,' said Alexander. 'How are you?'

'Well enough, I suppose,' answered the robot in melancholy tones.

'What's wrong, Endeepee?' asked Alexander. In fact he could guess the answer already.

Alexander had been part of the team which designed the NDP series. NDP-578 was a typical Mechanical Friend, designed to serve, look after and play with the average child. Endeepee had been a special present to Alexander's son, Harold. He had proved very useful for over three years of service. Now, however, Harold was in hospital after a fall from a tree and Endeepee was bored and lonely. He said so.

'I'm bored. I've got nothing to do.'

After a short pause, Alexander's trained mind came up with a solution.

'Why don't you watch some video tapes from the library. You can use my library card.'

Thousands of pulses crossed Endeepee's brain in a nanosecond (i.e. 10^{-9} of a second, a flash to the layman) to produce the answer, 'Thanks, I think I'll try that.' With that he slunk off. His manner did not betray his feelings, but then, how could it? Metal shoulders could not sag.

*

When Harold returned home six days later, he was not disturbed to find Endeepee by a pile of thirteen tapes of *Solar Protector Blake*, a popular super-hero. It was only the following week that trouble arose.

Harold was watching his favourite TV programme. Endeepee, in his capacity as child minder, stood by expressionlessly. A sudden newsflash interrupted the programme. It warned of 'suspected pirate space-ships on the Earth–Venus trade route'. After the newsflash ended, Endeepee turned to Harold and spoke in a strangely low voice. 'Somewhere in our galaxy evil lurks, disturbing men's lives. It's another amazing mission for Solar Protector Blake!' With that he turned and ran (or rather drove) off.

'No, Endeepee! Come back!' implored Harold. 'Please!' Heedlessly Endeepee clambered up the stairs to the roof (10 metres high). He spread his numerous arms (all eight), and rushed to the roof's edge. Flailing his arms uselessly, he fell and shattered. From the mangled robot body, a small metallic voice still issued: 'On a mission to save the Earth, our mechanical superhero ... mechanical super ... mechanical su ... me–cha–ni–cal ...'

On 17 June 2157 the NDP robot series was taken out of circulation, compensation being promised by the manufacturers to the owners. Human superheroes can be tolerated, but mechanical ones?

5

The Swamp Child

Joanna Freyther

CHAPTER 1

The rain had ceased. The sun crept out guiltily from behind a drained cloud and gave a gentle glow of yellow warmth. 'At last,' I shouted, and ran downstairs to get my coat. More haste, less speed, I reminded myself as I rebuttoned my coat. Finally I struggled into my shoes, unlocked the front door and stepped out into the damp garden. A smell of damp cut grass and wet earth rushed to greet me.

Trotting across the deserted road I shooed a few brown hens back into the stable yard. They squawked and rumbled disagreeably, not wishing to lose a meal of worms from the gardens. 'Off with you!' I shouted as I continued down the path to the marshy, swampy woods. The nettles had sprung up suddenly on each side, along with clumps of cow parsley. The hawthorn which had covered the trees for weeks with its snowlike appearance was starting to turn a pale pink, and somewhere a cockerel crowed. The narrow path was muddy and slippery after the rain and twice I nearly slipped, so I slowed my feet to a reasonable pace.

As I entered the wood two geese on my left hissed and honked as I passed their pond. 'Boo!' I shouted, and jogged on round the corner. On the right flowed the river – a smooth, calm, blue ribbon fringed by grasses and leafy trees. The land on my side was quite different. It was a dark wood with sucking, stagnant swamps and spindly green trees which grew in among ivy and bindweed. I had decided to go through the woods to the bridge, because even though I hated this eerie wood it was the quickest way to the bridge. A nettle stung me so I stopped to pick a dock leaf to calm my bitten leg, and then I saw the child.

CHAPTER 2

The child was not very tall, about 4 feet, quite thin and looking straight at me with owl-like eyes. My hand froze, even my leg stopped stinging. I was firmly rooted into the ground. The child didn't look at all frightened; its eyes just got bigger and rounder. I decided the child couldn't hurt me so I just stepped back slightly and carried on staring. It was a girl with long brown hair and a thin face. Her skin was slightly green and she had a cloth round her waist. She was not totally human – her hands and feet were webbed and she was green all over.

From the other side of the river came a sharp yap. I spun round to see a small spotty dog looking over the river at us. When I turned back the girl was gone, and the only movement was a trail of bubbles along the swamp's surface. Surely not, I thought, but the girl had definitely gone. 'No,' I said again. 'Never!' and ran back home.

I slept badly that night and woke up early next morning. Once again I walked down to the woods, wondering if what I had seen was true. Along the path I went, past the noisy geese and round the corner to the swamp. There she was, collecting leaves and nettles with her webbed hands. Hearing me, she turned to face me and smiled. I smiled back, less frightened now but still apprehensive. Then the girl said, 'Yarna.'

Supposing that was her name, I answered, 'Joanna.'

'Come,' she said, and beckoned with a webbed finger.

I followed the girl along an overgrown path, past the swamp and into a tree cave. We sat down on rotting logs. Yarna whistled and through the trees came a grey heron and a little brown frog. 'Garni,' said Yarna, pointing at the frog and pointing at the heron, she said, 'Krena.' I nodded, unsure and studied both animals while Yarna prepared some leaves in a clay pot. The frog was a common type with bright eyes, but the heron was only knee-high.

CHAPTER 3

We became very good friends. Yarna taught me many secrets of nature, and I learned to understand Garni and Krena, and even how to make their meals. I wondered how much longer this friendship would last. You can't keep a swamp child secret. Twice I almost let it slip out. One Monday morning I was going to see Yarna when my mum asked, 'Where are you off to?'

I replied, 'Off to the woods to see Yarna.'

'Who's Yarna?' she had said.

'Oh, just a frog,' I answered quickly, blushing red.

The next day at school I wrote a message on my hand, YARNA, TONIGHT 7.30.

'Who's Yarna?' Emily asked.

'Oh, just a friend.'

Emily stared suspiciously and whispered something to Kirsty. I told Emily the next day at school about Yarna and asked her not to tell. In bed that night I felt terrible. Why had I told her? From then on I kept my mouth shut, but the damage was done, the secret was out. In a week most of the school knew. I told them I had been pretending but they didn't believe me.

One morning I went back to the swamp. Something was wrong. The geese were quiet and the birds twittered uneasily. The soft ground at the edge of the swamp was pitted with footprints, some large and heavy, and some . . . webbed.

CHAPTER 4

'Yarna,' I called. 'Yarna.' There was no answer, just a bird circling in the sky above. And then I knew she had gone for ever, been taken away to a laboratory, to be cut up alive just for the sake of money. And it was all my fault. I ran deeper and deeper into the woods, tears streaming from my eyes, my legs shaking. I ran on with the awful guilt that I had killed her. She had died because of me and my stupid mouth.

Later on in the year I went down to the swamp again. The geese still hissed and the spindly trees still grew in green confusion. Nothing's changed, I thought, but rounding the corner to the swamp, I realized how wrong I was. It would never be the same here. Never the same without Yarna.

12 May 2030

Michael McKenna

08.00
Got up and got dressed in my anti-radiation suit. Went and put on my deodorant. Didn't bother buying Ozone Friendly because there is no ozone to be friendly to.

09.00
Went out to my shuttle to go up to the special school in space, up above the atmosphere, so that we wouldn't be fried by the Greenhouse Effect.

10.00
We did some history, on the Earth, 1980 to 2000. Seems they didn't care much about the environment then, although some of the governments did try to promote lead-free petrol and ozone-friendly aerosols.

12.00
Got out of school early because a meteor hit the physics lab. Flew down in my shuttle to the sausage and chips shop. It used to be called a fish and chips shop, but with all the pollution in the water finding a fish would be like finding a gold-mine.

15.00
It started raining so I had to find shelter quick. What's wrong with a bit of rain, you may ask. Well, it's acid

rain, so if you don't find shelter quick you'll be like a fried egg.

18.00
Turned on the TV to see the news and weather. The weatherman said, 'Floods are expected in the Belfast area and a hurricane is heading towards London. Acid rain is expected in the Midlands and Northern Ireland.'

21.00
Went to bed and dreamt about the world being green and pleasant. Huh! Some hope after the people fifty years ago messing this planet of life, the Earth, up.

Nigel

Peter Moore

There once lived an owl in the days of old who sang all day and night. If anyone dared to listen they would do something drastically horrible.

Nigel the owl lived in an old humble forest where many an owl had lived before. Nigel was a barn owl. Many knights had attempted to sellotape his beak up, but none had succeeded. The king had declared that the person who sellotaped up the owl's beak could marry the princess, his daughter.

There was a young boy from Derby named Fred who was a very poor young lad who so clearly had a heart of fire for the admirable princess. One day he rode down to London on his mule to have a go at Sellotaping the owl's beak up.

'Are you mad?' asked the king.

'I don't think so,' replied Fred.

'Do you think that a little boy like you could do a task like this? Ha, ha, ha!'

Fred didn't care what the king said. Fred was determined to sellotape Nigel's beak up whatever the king said to him.

The next day Fred went to the forest to find the owl. He stumbled through the forest jumping the branches, when he heard someone sneeze!

'A – A – CHOO!'

'Are you all right, dear friend?' Fred asked a little squirrel sneezing constantly.

'Well, you see ... AaaaCHOOOO!' said Sally squirrel. 'I've got this dreadful prob – Aaaaa-CHOOOOOOO! – problem!'

'I see,' said Fred. 'Is there anything I can do for you?'

'Well, as a matter of fact you can do something. Will you get me a branch out of an old oak tree, dip it in a lake and thrust the solution up my nostrils?'

'All right, but whatever do you want me to do that for?' Fred said, foolishly, but then he soon remembered. 'Oh, of course, stupid of me, it stops you coughing!' remarked Fred.

'Nearly,' said the squirrel. 'Actually it's to do with sneezing!'

Fred did what he was asked.

Soon he was back.

'Here you are,' said Fred.

'Thank you,' said Sally.

'What purpose are you in the forest for?' asked Sally.

'I am attempting to sellotape Nigel's beak up. So that I can marry the princess,' said Fred.

'I can help you there,' said Sally. 'If you collect the ears of seven spiders and put them in a wooden bowl with fish blood, then drink half of it and put the other half in your socks, it will stop you doing something silly when you have heard the owl sing, though it will still sound horrible!' With that, off ran the squirrel.

Fred put the bowl under his left arm, and continued along the footpath.

Fred bumped into a hedgehog, moaning under a fence by the side of the footpath.

'Help! Help!' cried the poor animal. 'Help!'

'It's OK,' said Fred. 'What can I do for you, my friend?'

'Well, could you pull this thorn out of my paw and get me out of this trap?' yelled the hedgehog.

'Fine, anything you want, my friend.'

'Please,' said the hedgehog, 'please call me Henry. My real name is Harry, but I would prefer it if you called me Henry.'

'All right, Henry,' said Fred.

Fred pulled the thorn out of Henry's paw and cut the rope in the trap with his pocket penknife.

'I must be off,' said Henry. 'But if there's anything at all you want, do tell me now.'

'Well, there is in fact. Do you know how I could catch the singing owl and sellotape his beak up?'

'That is a coincidence,' said Henry. 'I have an owl detector!'

Henry gave Fred his owl detector, and scampered off through the long grass back to his family.

The next day Fred woke up to find himself at the heart of a jumble sale. He saw a pair of magic headphones and some sellotape which he bought with a shilling.

He took the special set of headphones which would make the owl's singing pleasant and the sellotape, to sellotape up Nigel's beak.

Continuing his quest, he met up with his old friend Mathew mole. Mathew mole was hiking up a tree trunk with his mountaineering equipment. They had a cup of lemon tea and a chat.

'I've been tree hiking for several years now,' said Mathew. 'It's my hobby.'

'Well, at the moment I'm planning on marrying the princess,' said Fred.

'Who's a lucky boy, then, hey!' said Mathew.

'Well, not just yet because I need to catch the singing owl first,' said Fred. 'I just need some rope to make a trap, and some more to tie Nigel up with.'

'I've got loads of rope,' said Mathew. 'How do you think I do tree hiking, huh?'

Mathew gave Fred all his spare rope.

Fred put all his gear on and filled his socks with half of his solution, and the rest he drank in one gulp. He started searching for the owl. First he bumped into a tawny owl, but then he found Nigel. It was a desolate place and very creepy.

Fred set up his trap on the tree nearby. Fred couldn't wait, but in the end, Nigel flew into the trap and Fred pulled the rope tightly from underneath the tree. Nigel was flapping his wings desperately like a maniac. Nigel was trying to cut the rope with his claws, but it was extremely strong rope. (It had to be for mountaineering, you couldn't take any chances.)

Nigel started singing but that didn't work either.

Fred tied his end of the rope to a huge tree trunk. He chased Nigel around the tree so he wouldn't have any rope left to fly about on. Fred Sellotaped the rope to the tree trunk firmly and then sellotaped Nigel's beak up.

Nigel tried to bite Fred but did not succeed. Now the deed was done, Fred cut the rope by the Sellotape. He used the same pocket penknife which he had used to set Henry free.

On the way back he said goodbye to all his friends again that he'd met on this exciting journey.

The king had no choice but to let Fred marry Isabel, his daughter.

At the wedding Fred didn't forget to invite all his friends, the squirrel, Henry and the jumble sale's assistant. If it hadn't been for them, then he wouldn't have been standing where he was now.

As he had known Mathew the longest, because he was an old friend, Mathew was the best man.

Fred cut the cake with the same pocket penknife that he had made the trap with and set free Henry with.

Fred and Isabel went to Queensland for their honeymoon that same day, so it isn't hard to guess that everyone lived Happily Ever After.

Milly Mole Takes Off

Polly Findlay

Milly Mole was baking crumpets. Her crumpets were scrummy. When they had been baked, Milly decided to have a nice, long walk while the crumpets cooled. She poked her nose out. 'Hmm,' she said. 'I think I smell burning fuel.' She was right. There was an old rocket.

'Ooh,' she said, when she found the door. It was very round. It was not locked, so she went inside. It was nice and warm and had a big red seat. It looked very cosy so she sat on it. It was not cosy at all. In fact, it was cold and smooth and bouncy. 'Dear me,' she said, 'what a funny seat!'

Suddenly the rocket began to move. Suddenly, she knew she had sat on the blast-off button! 'Ooh,' she said, 'I'm going to Mars!'

But she was not going to Mars. She was going to the Moon. But that was exciting enough! There was an old spacesuit with some oxygen in the tank. Milly put it on. She looked very smart!

She had a peek out of the window. 'Ooh,' she gasped, for there, in front of her, there was SPACE! 'Ooh,' she said again. 'Well, I'd better get ready. I'll be arriving at the Moon, not Mars!' Then there was a soft bump and Milly was on the Moon.

'That was quick,' cried Milly. She got out. It was

black all around her. Then she looked down at her feet. The ground was white. It had funny holes in it called craters.

'What fun!' Jump, bounce, jump, bounce.

But after a few days in Space she felt bored and lonely.

One morning she heard the sound of birds from Earth. One of them flew right up to Space for a holiday. He asked her why she was so lonely and glum. So she told him how she had baked the crumpets and found the rocket.

Then she told him how she had sat on the blast-off button.

'And now here I am,' she sighed.

'I understand,' said Roly Poly Rupert (for that was his name). 'I will take you back home,' said Rupert.

'Yes please!' cried Milly.

'Sure thing,' said Rupert.

'Great!' said Milly. 'How much will it cost?'

'Nothing except a packet of birdseed,' he said.

'Fine,' said Milly.

'Right,' he said. 'Get on my back.'

'OK,' said Milly.

So off they went. Milly was amazed how quick they were. They were home in about one hour.

Roly Poly Rupert got his bag of seed. When he had gone, Milly got herself some tea and ate the crumpets.

My Soul

Eleanor Broadbent

To my parents, brothers and sisters –
Mummy, Daddy, Julia, Gavin, Edmund, Frankie,
Alexis, Amalia, Gregory, Ralph
and baby Abigail

I was an ant once. It was horrid. In danger of being killed every second, we were so small we were hardly part of the world. My home was a nest made up of lots of chambers and passages. Our leader, the queen, had a chamber of her own and there were separate other rooms for the little ones – the eggs, the larvae and the pupae. All our rubbish was kept in a different room still. When it was too hot or too cold we changed the temperature by opening or closing some of the passages. Thousands of us lived together but I always felt different because of my bigger soul. We each had different tasks – to collect food, to care for the eggs or larvae, to repair the nest or guard it. My job was to collect food – the delicious honeydew on plants.

My friend was a queen. She went off to start a new nest. She bit off her wings, then found a little hole where she laid her eggs. I missed her a lot.

Great big things hung over and trod on us. My mum was lost like that. One of the things poured boiling water on us. They did not like us but I wanted to like them.

There was an object that flew. It was a great mystery how it could do that. The object kept sweeping down and eating us ants. So many things did not like us it made me cry.

The object that flew was flying over my house. It picked me up and ate me. I had such a big soul I took over the flying object. Later I discovered that the object was called a bird.

At first it was difficult. There was so much to learn. I could not make nests. Collecting bits of straw and balancing in the tree was hard. Somehow I could not get the hang of it. So I found another bird's nest and laid my egg there. I tipped out one of the bird's own eggs. Then I felt better but sad to know I would not see my own egg hatch. You probably realize I was a cuckoo.

I liked flying. Looking down on the green ground, field after field, searching for food, was a pleasure. But humans kept trying to kill us for a sport. I think it was called hunting. The hunters were aiming at bigger birds but we got in the way. I did not approve of it.

Once I came across a huge animal. I thought I could eat it so I attacked. The fox was much bigger and stronger. It ate me. I had such a big soul I took over that animal as well.

Now I was something which came out at night when everyone else was asleep. It was dead quiet and not a sound to disturb the stillness of the night. I had to learn to hunt but I never liked to kill. My main foods were ground squirrels, mice, insects and fruit. I especially liked blackberries but I used to eat anything. My face was pointed, my fur and tail thick. I lived in an earth. When I first heard the word I did not realize it meant my home.

Soon I liked being a fox, except I had no friends. Another thing disturbed me. Hunting. The human hunting was horrible. Packs of dogs and men in red coats on horses would chase me for miles until I could escape into a deep hole. Of course, eventually I was caught. A little boy was blooded with me. I felt sorry for him because my soul was such a big soul I knew it would take over his life. So I took over the boy and became a human.

I never killed again. I became a vegetarian, which was satisfying, and spent my time raising money to protect wildlife. I often wonder how many other 'people' like me there are in the world.

The Dragon's Shadow
That Was Stolen

Andrea Jones

In a cave dark and gloomy sat a dragon, a dragon with a shadow which he never let out of his sight.

In a land there lived a shadow-nicker. He had a big black sack that hung over his shoulder and a big black cloak which drooped over his back.

One foggy night when the shadow-nicker was on duty, he passed the dragon's cave. Then he stopped and went inside.

Inside lay the dragon fast asleep with his shadow hung up on the wall. The shadow-nicker took the shadow off the wall, careful not to rip it.

In the morning the dragon went to put his shadow on but it wasn't there. He looked all around his cave – in tins and books because sometimes it liked to hide. He thought about what his friends had told him about the shadow-nicker. He hadn't believed them but now he wasn't sure.

He asked his friends where the shadow-nicker lived. Some said north and some said south. But one said: 'In a dark street in a dustbin.'

'But which street?' he asked.

'No one knows,' he said.

The search began. He looked high and low, but not a thing.

On the way he met all kinds of creatures, like the

three-eyed wombat, the gooly granny monster, and, last of all, the slobbish monster.

They all joined the line.

The three-eyed wombat had three eyes and hung upside-down. The gooly granny monster had her hair up in a big grey bun. But as for the slobbish monster, he just had slobbish thoughts.

CRASH! A bin overturned. They looked inside and saw the dragon's shadow amongst other shadows. There were shadows of hearts, leaves and the Moon. But as for the shadow-nicker, he got lost in his own shadows.

Out for the Day

Blake Ritson

Plink! A sunbeam poured into the glass of ice-cold, twice as nice cold partlejuice as Kalbé fumbled for the touch control on the alarm. Plink! Plink! The alarm beeped on and on as his half-numbed, sleepy fingers failed to connect. The vid-screen sang.

> Wake up, wake up, it's a lovely day!
> It's time to be up and on your way.

Its cheery, metallic voice filled the sleeping compartment as a hologram of sand and a deep, blue sea washed over the small, sleepy figure.

'Go away,' he mumbled. 'I need my sleep, I'm growing.'

> No excuses, time for fun,
> My, you are a sleepy one,

chirped the screen as a row of palm trees materialized on the south wall.

'I'm sure it's time I had an adult vid-screen,' protested Kalbé, angrily rubbing his eyes. 'I'm too old for all this rubbish.'

> It's your last call, last call,
> Pride goes before a fall,

sang the screen, as his sleep-capsule rose into the air

43

and tilted sharply, dropping him in a crumpled, angry heap on the floor. He hardly had time for a rude reply before the entrance panel slid open and his pet robot, Obé, entered carrying a tray of carefully balanced vitamin and mineral tablets for breakfast. Simultaneously the seaside scene dissolved and in its place stood his parents and rather irritating small sister, Kcenniniap.

'Come on, Kalbé, you're late,' said his mother. 'Don't you remember, today we're going to Fortunata Adventureland?'

'Why is it always you we're waiting for?' shouted Kcenniniap.

Kalbé shrugged and called after them as they walked off into the distance, 'Sorry, I really won't be long, I'll meet you at the arrival pad.'

They were swiftly replaced by assorted aerial views of Fortunata Adventureland, accompanied by an oozing description of all its attractions. Kalbé gulped the tablets, had a quick laser shower, patted Obé and in no time at all was standing on the transportation pad outside his compartment. As he punched in the coordinates he felt a twinge of excitement. He just knew that today was going to be really big.

The sun shone invitingly down on the crowded park, picking out the garish aerial laser displays hovering in mid-air, advertising each attraction.

'We're going to the Black Hole of Terror first,' yelled his sister, hopping about in front of him as Kalbé materialized on the entrance pad. 'Come on, Kalbé, you're late.'

With their eyes fixed on the black, gaping hole in the sky advertising the park's latest attraction, the family made their way through the brightly coloured walkways. They passed the display of ancient space vehicles and stopped for a quick ride on the anti-grav roller coaster.

'I feel like my insides have been scrambled,' shuddered his sister excitedly. 'Let's go on it again.'

'No,' said their father firmly, 'the crowds are going to be vast at the Black Hole of Terror. We must get there early or we will have to queue all day.'

They hurried on. The walkway grew narrower and less well kept. Finally it ended at an enclosure occupied by a sad-looking family of animals surrounded by a crowd of spectators.

'Oh no,' groaned Kcenniniap, 'we've taken a wrong turning. We'll never . . .'

The rest of her sentence was lost as the crowd gasped with horror and astonishment.

'What is it?' Kalbé asked his father.

'Come along,' he said briskly, 'we don't need to watch this. It's feeding time.' He shuddered.

One of the creatures was actually hacking slices from a charred, dead animal and placing them in the feeding bowls. He added pieces of mutilated vegetation which seemed to have gone through a similar heating process. The feeding bowls were handed round and the family ate. They actually looked as though they were enjoying this nauseating concoction.

45

The crowd groaned and many of them stumbled away, looking sick.

'Revolting!' said Kalbé's mother. 'Most unsuitable. Come along, children.'

'Can't we just stay for a little while?' pleaded Kalbé. There was something strangely fascinating about the pathetic little group.

'Come on, Kalbé, we'll be late,' shrieked his sister, exasperated.

'You go. I'm staying.' He shook her off. He turned to his parents. 'Can I stay, please? I won't be long and I'll meet you at the Black Hole of Terror.'

'Very well, if you must,' said his father. 'I suppose the worst is over. Just don't be too long.'

The crowd was beginning to drift away as Kalbé approached the enclosure. He stared hard at the creatures. They were a family just like his – a mother, father and a young male and female. The young male looked about the same age as him. He walked to the front of the enclosure and stared at Kalbé. It was funny, but he could have sworn the creature looked intelligent. Kalbé put his hand against the transparent wall and to his surprise the small creature put his up to meet it. He put the other hand up and again the little creature matched his movement. Laughing, he copied Kalbé as he jumped up and down. He looked so innocent and trusting; their eyes met, but it was Kalbé's eyes which fell first as he turned and walked away.

'They shouldn't lock them up for people to stare

at,' he muttered. 'It's not right. They should be free like we are.'

A cloud passed across the sun and the fun and brightness disappeared from the day, leaving Kalbé with a cold, uncomfortable feeling in the pit of his stomach. He wandered off towards the woods behind the enclosure, down a tiny, overgrown path used by the keepers. He banged angrily at the back of the enclosure and was amazed to see it move. A large panel was loose. He tugged and pulled, it came away in his hands . . .

The Black Hole of Terror was totally terrifying and well worth the terrible wait. Kalbé enjoyed it, but while the family soared and dipped on the Cloud Chaser he sat thoughtfully in his seat and did not seem to notice the ride. The Living Past Museum of Ancient Transport, filled with old cars, trains, boats and aeroplanes, which made absolutely everyone laugh, left him looking blank. He hardly noticed the fearful phantoms in the Ghostly Castle. It was only in the mind-boggling, pin-zingling Magnetic Needlestorm Voyage of a Lifetime that he finally looked as though he was enjoying himself. It did, however, take an awful lot of time afterwards to remove all the needles.

It had been a good day. The exhausted family was grouped around the vid-screen in their living compartment watching the news.

'It has been reported from Fortunata Adventureland that, due to a structural defect in their enclosure in the Endangered Species Area, a family of creatures has escaped. Sadly, they could not live outside their controlled environment and they have perished in our atmosphere. They were the last known examples of the creatures who inhabited our planet many hundreds of years ago. They were the last of the human race. Now sport . . .'

Kalbé dug his claws hard into the thick floor-covering as a large golden tear trickled down his scarlet scales.

Wart Went to Pendle

Patrick M. Granger

One night, when I was asleep, my wart decided to go and live at Pendle Hill. So it jumped off my thumb, ran across the bedroom carpet and went down the stairs. Then it climbed out through the letterbox into the garden. It was very dark in the garden. The moon was in the sky, and all the stars were out and the street lamps were on and my wart went all the way to Pendle Hill. How did it get there? Well, I think it went on a Massey Ferguson tractor. But there was a witch at Pendle Hill and she wanted to make my wart into soup, so he ran all the way back home and got back on my thumb. But the next morning, the skin on my hand smelt just the same as before, as if my wart had never been away.

The Python, the Boa
and Friends

Jane Jeffrey

One day in the reptile house the boa said to the python, 'I'm bored of being stuck in this cage. I want to see the world.'

'I would settle for the rest of this zoo,' said the python.

'Well, what are we waiting for?' cried the boa.

'These are glass cages. How do we get out?'

'We are strong constrictors, you know. We'll smash our way out.'

Smash, smash, crack, crash, bash.

'We're out,' cried the python. 'So this is the great outdoors.'

'Shush, not so loud,' said the boa. 'Come on, let's slip out of the reptile house and have fun. Let's go and see Trunky the elephant.'

Off they went to the elephant house.

'Here we are,' said the python. 'It's a bit crowded.'

'Never mind,' said the boa, 'we can bite the people in the way. Let's climb up this wall first and see the turtles, then let's see Trunky.'

'Hi,' said Tom the turtle. 'What are you doing here? You should be in the reptile house.'

'It's a long story,' said the boa. 'It's nice to see you again but we must be going because we're on the way to see Trunky.'

A man got in the way so the boa bit him!

'Ow!' said the man. 'You shouldn't go round biting people.'

At the elephant house they saw Trunky.

'Hello,' said Trunky. 'I wouldn't stay around here too long. The keeper's coming soon.'

'We'd better get out of here,' said the boa.

'Bye,' said the python.

So off they went back to the reptile house.

Sixth Sense

Hannah Pennell

Michael fingered his box of Technical Lego, feeling downcast at his Christmas present. He realized with a start that he had been right. His inner mind had told the truth.

Last night, on Christmas Eve, Michael had lain by the fire, lazily stroking the ginger cat, Champagne, while his younger sister, Alice, danced round Grandpa, pestering him with dreams of the cuddly polar bear which she had noticed displayed in the toyshop window. Although he had not been told, Michael suddenly, vividly, knew that she was going to get it. He could see the bear, staring pathetically with melting brown eyes. Around it lay blue wrapping paper patterned with snowy villages. He shook himself. Then he tested his imagination regarding his own present. Again he saw a vision, this time of a box of Technical Lego wrapped in green.

Now, on Christmas Day, he stood holding the Technical Lego with a scrap of green paper in his hand. Alice, in the corner, cooed over a polar bear surrounded by village wrapping paper and insisted on showing him to everyone: Aunt Rose, Uncle Peter and Grandpa. She hugged the cuddly bear while she paraded him round. Michael fumed inwardly, although he did not know why. Lunch was better.

Everyone had seen the turkey being prepared. Nothing was surprising in knowing what was for lunch. But still lunch was difficult. Michael knew he would have a red cracker sealed with a plum pudding and he knew that inside he would have a cracked pink beetle with shifty eyes. (Alice took the beetle and annoyed him by waving it around 'to test the wobbliness of its eyes'.)

His power worried him, but it was not until he was in bed thinking over the strange happenings of the day that he managed to untangle the mysterious happenings. He had tried to hold Alice, on the afternoon walk, to stop the nagging feeling that she would fall in the river, but she had thought him silly and skipped on. She had returned bedraggled and wet. He wondered until he fell asleep.

This power kept reappearing and Michael was scared to think of the future. Term started. Michael had an idea that something as down-to-earth as school would prevent him from predicting. Still his ability to visualize the future remained. He found out irritatingly small things – his Valentine's card had been sent by Jennifer Colley; his raffle tickets were useless, he knew they were not going to win; even his birthday treat, a surprise trip to the circus, was spoilt, he knew he was going beforehand.

Walking home from school Michael explored a new point of view concerning his power. It was odd how it had suddenly arrived. Before Christmas he had expected and enjoyed surprises. The guessing and excitement leading up to events had been part of the fun. Now the pleasure had been taken away from treats because of the knowledge of the expedition beforehand. He was scared of his strong future-telling power, scared to look into the future, but compelled to think of what was to come. Then at once Michael knew why he had clairvoyant power. His ability would not have just come without some reason behind it: it was a warning. His mind turned over earthquakes, firebombs and other exotic disasters, mostly inspired by television, and then dis-carded them. Here, in Grove Street, real life was lived. He tried to think hard, hoping for a vision of the disaster about to overwhelm him, but all he saw in his mind's eye was his mother cooking fish and chips for a special tea. He crossed the road carefully, waiting for the lights to change in his favour, and turned in at his gate. As he opened the back door the smell of frying fish wafted on the breeze.

A few weeks later Michael had the first of a series of nightmares. Each night he had a terrifying vision and each night his mother spent almost half an hour comforting and reassuring him. By day, too, some-thing he could not define kept him alert and watchful. He would not be left alone but followed his mother around the kitchen and house. His mother felt there was something strange and inquired before bedtime, but, as she later reported to her husband, over television and tea, 'He just snapped back at me that there was nothing wrong, and asked me to leave him alone, in such a way that I knew straightaway that something was wrong.'

As the two parents settled more comfortably on the cushioned sofa and fixed their eyes on the TV film, Michael tossed and turned upstairs, but decided not to tell his mother anything. If she laughed at his fears and fantasies as nonsense, he would feel humiliated; if she believed him, far worse, he would realize that his power carried force. As the days went by Michael subsided into an inhibited silence.

On 22 February matters reached a climax. Alice had departed for Susan's house, where the attractions of a litter of noisy puppies outweighed those of her own house, empty with its quietness. Father, too, had left the kitchen and begun a new program on the computer. The time would have been ideal for Michael's mother to ask him what the matter was, and she paused indecisively, not knowing how to begin. In the silent kitchen the mechanical hum of the computer in the next room sounded loud. She had by now become accustomed to the sulky silence, but was startled to hear the stifled sound as Michael, unable to keep up his strike, began to cry. Using kind, comforting words she managed to bring him to coherent speech. Like a stream in spring the words tumbled out, at first a few ideas and hints, then swollen to a torrent as Michael related his dreams and fears and declared his amazing clairvoyance.

Later Mrs Amon confessed to her husband that she did not believe a word of it, all teenage exaggeration and too much television. But this episode provided a background for the astonishing command that Michael gave the family a week later.

On 1 March, a dull day, returning from school, Michael was aware of a pressure in his mind. He felt as if his mind was on fire, each flame licking round still undefined visions; each flame crackling with danger. He shook his head to try and clear the pictures, but they remained shadowy as figures round a bonfire. He went through the routine of everyday life: homework, tea, playing computer games. Nothing looked out of place, nothing hinted at disaster. He slotted 'Alien Attack' into the computer and tried to focus his mind on the game. Bleeps and explosions, crashes and safe landings, followed their random pattern; but the monochrome screen flashed red and yellow, dazzling his attention. Flickers of gold blurred the enemy movements. In his head he heard the roar of flames, the tinkle of breaking glass. He smelt the acrid smell of smoke and burning timber. Choking for breath, as if in a real inferno, Michael cried out, 'Out, get out of the house!'

Over and over he heard a voice he recognized as his own shrieking the warning. Catching the urgency in his voice his mother and sister fled, feeling his authority, and scared by his desperation.

Outside it was raining, with a mizzly rat-grey rain which was depressing. Alice hopped from foot to foot complaining, and Mrs Amon showed signs of moving back into the house, but the wind blew danger in the air and Michael restrained them.

An explosion: fire, timber, glass; for a few minutes there was a choking mass of smoke and rubble. As the smoke cleared, a flame licking high devoured the upstairs, and the roof fell in, spilling stored furniture into the inferno. Michael recognized his bedstead, still covered in football pictures, sticking awkwardly from the debris, and Alice's rocking horse was beside it, its wooden face smiling to the end.

The next day's *Daily Craven* carried the headline:

BOY SAVES FAMILY WITH UNCANNY NOTION
AS GAS BLAST DESTROYS THEIR HOME.

A Picture is Worth
a Thousand Words . . .

Haggai Scolnicov

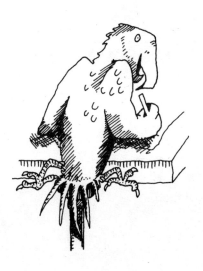

'You are a fool, John! Cerebral analysis is a useless field. It's hopeless. All languages must have a mathematical basis!'

'Perhaps, perhaps. But our new super-birds can grasp languages far better than a box of silicon-based circuits.'

'No! A parrot with smart grandparents can't bypass the intricacies of the biggest computers on earth just like that.'

'Fine. It can't. But I've had Captain Cook for three months and he can already identify thirty nouns. What has your computer done in twelve years?'

Despite the ceaseless argument between these two men, they were good friends. They were both working to achieve fuller understanding of human languages. John White, tall and dark-haired, believed that the brain's patterns were far too complex to copy into a computer, and that certain animals could be taught to speak. Thomas Mason, however, thought that enough electronic components could do practically anything man wanted.

The argument continued until they reached John's house. As he unlocked the door he explained to Thomas: 'He's a bit shy of strangers still. It may take some time to get him to perform.'

It didn't, as it turned out. Captain Cook was perching on the couch looking about him. He hadn't noticed them, and John signalled his friend for silence. Captain Cook flapped his wings and squawked: 'Chair!' Within seconds, he was on the chair. Again he called out: 'Table!' and flew to the table. He looked behind him and recognized his owner. 'John! John!' He beat his wings and flapped over to John's shoulder.

John pointed at his guest and said slowly: 'Thomas. Tho-mas.'

'Thomas! Thomas!' shrieked Captain Cook, then turned back to John. 'Food?' he inquired in a shrill voice.

'Yes. OK, greedy bird.'

He placed a plate of birdseed in front of him and turned to Thomas. 'Well, Thomas? What do you think now?'

'It works,' Thomas admitted grudgingly. 'But dogs also recognize sounds and people, don't they?'

'Yes, but they don't use words themselves. I've got a complete simplified language for the super-birds.'

'But why should it all work?'

'Breeding, really. We've been breeding intelligent parrots for years. Captain Cook has all the qualities for learning a new language. Super-birds could be amazing successes, and not only as pets. Who knows what they could do?'

'Wait a minute. They're only birds. They could never really understand people. Take humour, for example. Could a parrot ever tell a joke? Or understand one?'

'I know that. But they could have some personality.'

'Fine. We'll see if computers don't win out.'

'We will.'

The rest of the evening passed peaceably as Captain Cook displayed his talents.

A few weeks later, the two friends were again on their way to John's house.

'You've got to face it, Thomas. Language computation is a dead field. We'll be marketing super-birds in a year, unless we come up against an obstacle, of course.'

'But Captain Cook is a single case. How could you generalize from that? Anyway, super-birds could never be human. They would have no idea of art, humour and everything else which makes humans human.'

'You asked how. Very simple. One: we are finding out more and more about the genetic traits needed to understand languages. We can breed super-birds for those traits. Two: Captain Cook has already learned to use verbs and adjectives, and he is learning now to use pronouns. Surely, other super-birds can't be much slower.'

'It can't work, I tell you. There are too many problems. You don't even know if super-birds see themselves or others as individuals with different personalities.'

'Well, I'm sure most problems can be solved. For example, I've already reduced the squawkiness of the Captain's accent to a minimum.'

Thomas stroked his short beard. 'Perhaps you have found the right way. But a computer which could speak . . . that *would* be a useful invention. Surely your super-birds could perform only simple tasks?'

'Maybe. I really don't know yet.'

They had gone by John's house without noticing and had to retrace their steps. As soon as John opened the door, the Captain arrived in a flurry of red and blue wings. 'Hello, John! Hello, Thomas! Hello!' He looked about himself and added thought-fully, 'Good evening, gentlemen.'

John stroked his neck feathers slowly and asked, 'Captain want food?' The multi-coloured super-bird considered the question and answered: 'Yes. Captain want food.'

'No. "*I* want food,"' corrected John.

'Yes. *I* want food.'

'Good boy, Captain!'

A plate of sliced fruit appeared in order to satisfy Captain Cook's appetite. When he had finished, John looked at him carefully and said: 'Describe Thomas, please.'

'Yes. Describe Thomas, describe Thomas.' The Captain appeared to be in deep thought. 'White, big shirt . . . black trou-sers . . . green pul-lo . . . pul-lo . . . pul-lo-ver . . . black shoes . . .'

'Good. Now describe his face.'

'Yes. Face. Big face, Small . . . small green eyes . . . small nose . . . big . . . ears. Beard. Muss-sa-ssh . . . muss . . .'

'No, Captain. Moustache, mous-tache.'

'Moustache,' said the Captain, a bit too quickly. 'Yes.'

'Quite good,' commented Thomas. 'But super-birds can recognize only objects for which they have words. For example, the Captain didn't notice my spectacles.'

'Of course. *I* don't have spectacles. But we plan to teach him a lot more,' said John. 'You never know *quite* what is going on in the mind of a different creature . . . Excuse me, I must make some notes.'

'Please do,' said Thomas. He was reading John's notes on SELASBI: Simplified English Language for Super-Birds.

John couldn't find any paper. 'Where paper, Captain?'

'Captain take. Captain Cook bad bad bad.'

'Don't tell me!' whispered Thomas. 'A manic-depressive parrot!'

'Not bad, Captain. Good Captain. Captain Cook bring paper.'

'Captain take paper . . . and . . . pen-cil. Captain do . . . do . . . do . . . draw!' exclaimed the super-bird triumphantly.

'Well, well!' muttered Thomas in mock-admiration. 'An artist, eh?'

'Captain bring pic-ture to me. Yes?'

'Yes.'

The Captain fluttered off and returned with John's pencil and a sheet of paper in his beak.

'Very good, Captain Cook! Look, Thomas. It must have been very difficult for the Captain to use the pencil.'

On the paper was what could only be a picture of the Captain himself. His wings were wide open and his beak was open as well.

'Fantastic!' said Thomas. 'Get him to draw another one.'

'Fine. Captain, draw an-other pic-ture,' said John, pointing at the Captain's first picture. He handed him pencil and paper and sat down to observe.

It was impossible to see what the Captain was doing, because he kept moving about and flapping his wings. Thomas and John were content to wait. 'Fi-nish-ed!' announced Captain Cook shrilly. The language may have been English, but the screech was the Captain's heritage of his jungle ancestors. He deposited the paper carefully in John's lap and withdrew to perch on his shoulder.

'Good picture?' he inquired.

John could only nod his head. He was speechless. 'It's . . . incredible!. . .'

Thomas leaned over. 'Can I see . . .?' At last he was converted to John's views. 'A parrot with a sense of humour!'

There on the page was a full-sized sketch of

Captain Cook. On his left shoulder was perched a minute man. It was quite obviously the bespectacled Dr Thomas Mason, mouth gaping open and his arms flapping at his sides.

How the Flying Fox
Came to Fly

An unpublished Rudyard Kipling
'Just So Story', found by

Jonathan Wilson-Fuller

You see, my friend, the flying fox could not always fly, no indeed. It all began, you see, in the land of Megacrointompet, way back in the time of Petintom. At this time there was a small fox named Cap'n'trumpet, who liked to eat fruit.

From the time Cap'n'trumpet was weaned he had always liked fruit and this caused many problems. For you see, my friend, his mother, Cap, and his father, Trumpet, were deeply dismayed and repeatedly chastised him for his foolish behaviour. In fact, all his family chastised him and repeatedly called him 'Cap'n'trumpet, foolish fox!' Whenever Cap'n'trumpet heard them call his name and add 'foolish fox', he would sleekly, stealthily slink away and hide.

Then one day his Great Aunt saw him at the tip-top of a big-broad-bulging banana tree. There he was, silently sitting in a state of complete and total euphoria, eating big-broad-bulging bananas. Cap'n'trumpet was completely contented, with his plump friend Mr Bird sitting beside him eating the scraps. Had it not been for Mr Bird's daintily-dazzling-debonair-dance, Cap'n'trumpet's Great Aunt would never have noticed her carefully camouflaged nephew. But when she did spy the happy pair she vocalized like a volcano! She shouted her disapproval for the whole wide world to hear, but Cap'n'trumpet was oblivious. He was so used to abuse and scolding and ridicule that in his contentment, so high above the ground, he was temporarily out of reach, both physically and mentally.

Cap'n'trumpet wandered home full and contented, wanting only to crawl into his nice, comfortable, warm bed. But what a reception committee awaited him! His parent's faces were cold with anger, their stern voices filled with disgust and disenchantment, as they scolded him yet again. Pleadingly they questioned, 'Why ever would a fox eat bananas?'

Cap'n'trumpet had heard this question many times before and knew it was unwise to attempt to answer. The result was as always, 'Cap'n'trumpet, foolish fox'. Everyone seemed to be jeering at him.

The worst was still to come, for his Great Aunt was furious at his unfoxlike behaviour, and when she spoke in anger it came with the fury of a force-five gale and everyone shook as if the ground itself was trembling!

'Bananas! Bananas! When you could have eaten that nice plump bird! You are a disgrace,' she firmly announced, and then concluded, 'Cap'n'trumpet, foolish fox is too mild a name for you . . . You are a fool's fool!'

That night Cap'n'trumpet went to sleep to the jeering chant of his brothers and sisters:

Why ever would a fox eat fruit?
Why ever would a fox eat fruit?
Fruit would suit a foolish fox,
Cap'n'trumpet, foolish fox!
Foolish fox,
Foolish fox,
Cap'n'trumpet, foolish fox!

In the following weeks wherever Cap'n'trumpet went to eat fruit the chant of 'Cap'n'trumpet, foolish fox' was never far behind. Cap'n'trumpet felt neglected, sad and lonely. He felt the world was against him. Even his friend, Mr Bird, was not to be found.

Then one day, as Cap'n'trumpet was sleekly, stealthily slinking away to hide, he heard Mr Bird softly saying, 'Cap'n'trumpet, wise little fox, forgive my dance that brought you strife.'

From then on, and very much to Cap'n'trumpet's relief, things began to look brighter. He met new friends, the foxes' jeering no longer hurt, and no longer did he have to sleekly, stealthily slink away to hide.

His new friends held a party for him with lots of fruit. They gave him a cap and trumpet as a welcoming gift. Cap'n'trumpet was pleased, but he was absolutely delighted when the ruler, Petintom, walked over to investigate their happy party. Petintom was enjoying his afternoon stroll when he saw Cap'n'trumpet and Mr Bird dancing in the shade of the big-broad-bulging banana tree. Cap'n'trumpet looked so handsome in his cap and playing his truly-newly trumpet while Mr Bird danced in his daintily-dazzling-debonair style. Petintom walked briskly over to the happy party and when Cap'n'trumpet's friends told him what had happened to Cap'n'trumpet, Petintom felt sorry for him.

In the weeks that followed Petintom and Cap'n'-trumpet became firm friends, meeting every day in Petintom's high-walled garden. Cap'n'trumpet was very happy and his favourite fruit was that which grew in the high-walled garden.

Now you see, my friend, there are some things you need to know. Petintom's high-walled garden was always locked because of the mysteriously-magical fruit that grew there, and until Cap'n'trumpet blew his trumpet, the gates would stay that way. The fruit that grew inside the high walls was mysteriously-magical, for whoever ate it would have the ability to know where he was going, even when his eyes were shut or it was dark, and Cap'n'trumpet received that mysterious-magical gift!

One day Petintom became ill and, what's worse, the key to the gates of the high-walled garden was lost. Cap'n'trumpet blew his trumpet at the gates of the high-walled garden, but the gates stayed locked. He blew louder, but still they remained locked. So he slinked sleekly, stealily, sorrowfully away to return another day. But the gates still remained locked no matter how hard he blew his trumpet. He was worried, for he sensed something was very wrong with his friend Petintom.

Cap'n'trumpet pleaded with Mr Bird. 'You can fly, so please go to the royal palace and find out what has happened.'

Mr Bird's mission was successful and he reported, 'Petintom is very ill and is asking for you, Cap'n'-trumpet.'

'How can I see Petintom when I can't even get through the gates?'

'Over the wall,' replied Mr Bird without hesitation.

'You forget I can't fly,' wistfully stated Cap'n'-trumpet.

'But you will for I will teach you,' assured Mr Bird.

After festooning Cap'n'trumpet's limbs with leaves, he took him to a high cliff and showed Cap'n'-trumpet how to fly. At first Cap'n'trumpet felt shakily-shivery and silly. He was scared just to steadily step into space! Then, finally, with conviction and courage, he followed his friend as he steadily stepped into space and gently, gracefully glided down. It wasn't long before Cap'n'trumpet had learned to fly!

When Cap'n'trumpet finally gained enough skill to fly over the wall, it was already dark, so Cap'n'trumpet had to use his magical ability to find the palace. The guards were fast asleep so he got past them easily. When he did find Petintom, he was asleep as well, so Cap'n'trumpet crawled under the bed and waited till morning.

When Petintom woke, he was delighted to see

Cap'n'trumpet. Cap'n'trumpet told him that his leafy adornment was part of a flying kit that Mr Bird had given him. Petintom was most impressed. It was obvious to Cap'n'trumpet that Petintom was very ill, so he did not tell him about the problem with the gate to the high-walled garden.

During his visit Cap'n'trumpet became aware of the guards' dislike of him and their jealousy of his friendship with Petintom. He decided to visit Petintom only at night, when they were unlikely to see him.

As the days went by Cap'n'trumpet realized that the guards were plotting against him and he would have to be very, very cautious. He decided he had better dwell deep in the dark-dank-damp caves of Cantompar-ma. No one entered these caves, for they were the mysterious, misty mansion of Bat, the mysterious winged god of the night.

Cap'n'trumpet left the caves only at night to visit Petintom and to eat the mysteriously-magical fruit in the high-walled garden.

When Petintom had completely recovered, the guards were no longer openly hostile to Cap'n'trumpet. The key to the gates of the high-walled garden was miraculously found! But after what had happened in the past months, Cap'n'trumpet would not trust the guards, for he knew their visible acceptance of him was only to please Petintom. So Cap'n'trumpet continued to live deep in the dark-dank-damp caves of Cantompar-ma and only to come out at night.

This, my friend, is how the flying fox came to fly and why it is known today as a bat.

Pegasus

Sarah Johnson

Once upon a time there was a girl called Emma. She lived in Scotland in 1899. Then one day something happened which changed her whole life.

One night in midwinter, when the moonbeams sent rays of milky light over the snow scene which lay still under the stars, Emma, not being a good sleeper and having woken up a few minutes before, got out of bed, drew back the curtains, opened the window and breathed in the cool night air. She stayed looking out over the tranquil, frosty scene until suddenly something on the lawn caught her eye.

At first it looked just like a moonbeam but then it took on a distinctive form – that of a horse. No, it couldn't have! Yes, it did! This great milk-white horse had huge feathered wings which shone like the moon, as did the rest of his body. As Emma watched, it slowly spread its wings and majestically soared away across the twinkling sky. This was Emma's first meeting with Pegasus, but not her last, as you will see.

In the morning she thought it was all a dream, but then she noticed that the window was wide open and when she looked out, she saw hoof prints on the lawn, which convinced her that Pegasus had not been a dream. When she told her parents, they did not believe her and when she showed them the hoof prints, they said that one of the horses from the neighbouring farm must have escaped and got on to their lawn.

But Emma knew that she'd seen a flying horse. During the next few days Emma saw Pegasus again, but she never got close to him as he always flew off. Then one night she crept stealthily outside and managed to catch him unawares. He tried to fly off, but Emma was already clinging to his back. Eventually, he turned his beautiful head and gazed at her with his beautiful brown eyes. She felt his warm breath on her hand and his warm coat under her.

To her surprise Pegasus spoke. He said in a clear voice, 'I am Pegasus, a flying horse. I have waited for a long time to find someone who could ride me. At last I have found you and you must help me with my quest to find the unicorns of the Unicorn Valley and bring back the golden pear that only grows in their king's garden.'

Emma thought for a moment that she had heard his name, but she couldn't think where. She jumped on his back and they flew away through the stars towards the Unicorn Valley, which lay due south. A long while passed and Emma began to ache all over. Then she noticed a planet to her right and recognized it as Venus, the Morning Star. She breathed a sigh of relief and knew that dawn was near. Pink, fleecy clouds floated by and a glowing orange sun rose in the sky, which was slowly turning blue. Pegasus announced, 'The valley lies on the other side of those treacherous mountains you see ahead.'

They rose and rose until they soared over the peaks. Emma was terrified. Pegasus's strength was flagging and they barely missed the peaks. His wings did not beat so strongly. His chest heaved and flecks of foam appeared at the corners of his mouth.

When at last they alighted in the valley, they heard a great whinnying and the next moment a herd of unicorns appeared, with their silver horns glinting in the warm sunshine that shone over the valley. They greeted Pegasus in a friendly manner, but when he told them what he wanted, they were doubtful as to whether their king would grant this request. All the same, Pegasus and Emma were shown to his palace, which was glistening in the sun. It was made of marble and gold, and had splendid silver doors. The king was lounging on a couch of red velvet and the gold trough in the corner had a feed of hay and oats in it. The king finally agreed to see them.

When they told him their request the king flew into a rage. Sparks flew from his eyes. He pranced around, boring his horn into the wooden wall. In the end, he calmed down when he was told that Pegasus needed the pear to make a paint to repaint the stars, which was his job every 100 years. He said, 'I will give you a gold pear if you can find it before I whinny.' Pegasus and Emma agreed to this condition and, after a hearty meal, were escorted to the garden by the king's page.

By the time the king had finished having a bath in the crystal waters of his lake and munching apples in his orchard, they had found the pear, and when he had finished rolling in his clover meadow he gave the great whinny which summoned them to the palace.

When the king saw that they had found the pear, he was furious and set them a task to do. He said, 'Go and fill a phial with water of life from the fountain which lies 12 leagues yonder, beyond the glass mountain.'

When they arrived, they found that it was guarded by a huge serpent curled three times round the spring. He was covered in fiery red and electric-blue scales, each one the size of the hand of a man. On his back were silver spikes the height of a unicorn's horn. His eyes were cucumber green and out of his mouth full of razor-sharp teeth flicked a forked tongue of pure black. When he saw Pegasus he fled, for he was dreadfully afraid of feathers as they made him sneeze. As he slithered away, he gave a violent 'Achoo!' and caused a dreadful earthquake. Emma was jolted off Pegasus's back and nearly fell into a wide chasm which opened at their feet.

After they had filled the phial, they returned to the king. When he saw that it was full he gave them the pear and let them return home.

When Emma arrived she found that no one had noticed her absence. Pegasus gave her a little silver horse as a keepsake and said, 'If you are ever in trouble, rub this horse three times and call my name.

I promise to come to your aid.' Emma looked up and
noticed a dark space in the sky. Pegasus flew up and
up and filled the gap in the sky. So that was where
Emma had heard the name Pegasus. He was a con-
stellation.

Naughty Mr Nip-Nip

James Granger

This story is dedicated to Mrs Briscoe,
with thanks for teaching me
how to read and write

Patrick's brother had a toy crocodile. It had sharp little teeth and sprung jaws and it was called Mr Nip-Nip. Patrick was frightened of it because it came alive. It would sneak up behind him when he played Lego. It would lurk under his duvet and hide in his slippers.

Every night when Patrick was asleep his Dad would switch off the bedroom light to save electricity. Patrick would wake up in the dark. He would hear the lid of the animal box opening. He would hear the crocodile scuttle across the carpet. And he would feel Mr Nip-Nip nibbling his toes. Patrick would SCREAM and wake everybody up.

And so one day the naughty Mr Nip-Nip got put into the dustbin. Not having Patrick's toes to nibble, Mr Nip-Nip got very hungry, but fortunately there was a lot of food in the bin.

On the first day he ate Sam's left-over omelette. The next day he had Daddy's grapefruit peel. The day after that he found some cold baked beans. But on the fourth day there was no food left, not even a carrot-bone.

On the fifth day the crocodile was really hungry, when he heard somebody walking down the path. It was the binman.

The binman took the lid off the bin and Mr Nip-Nip sprang out like a ballistic missile, snapping his jaws with evil intent.

The binman was so frightened he dropped his bin liner and ran down the path screaming. He jumped into the cab of his bin lorry and shut the door very quickly. The crocodile followed him and stood with his paws against the door, looking in through the window. Then he smelled the rubbish in the bin lorry. It smelled of fish and rotten fruit.

'Left-over NINS,' he said. 'Yum yum.'

He waddled round to the back of the lorry and jumped in. Very sneakily the binman got out of the cab and crept round to the back and pressed the button which started the crusher.

But the crocodile saw the blades coming and jumped over them. Then he ate the binman up and pigged all of the rubbish. And then he ran away to hide in someone else's bin. It could be yours.

The Forbidden Castle

David Harvey

The Dark Lord now rules the shattered world of Rhyce and only a small group of rebels dare to defy him. But although Rhyce is now a land of blackness and the Dark Lord has many spies, the rebels, known as the Troopers, have many allies from all races. The Fuzz, a furry lot; Trogs, an ogre-like bunch; Splods, who have no body and just a head, arms and legs; Freewheelers; and Humans. They must trek to the forbidden castle of Stokesay and win it back for the good of the folk of Rhyce. There will be no more terrorism of Troopers' farms or Troopers being tortured, no more trips to the dreaded maze if they regain control of the castle and Rhyce.

The mist came down on the castle as the last of the king's servants were ushered out of the gatehouse by the impatient goblins and creatures of the new king, the evil king! He was named the Dark Lord by the people of this land, for wherever he went became dark and dull. Poppies reeled over, roses became ash and oak trees crumbled as if a giant hand were pushing them over, and, worst of all, animals died and people began to starve. But the Dark Lord lived in luxury and pestered the farmers for what crops they had left.

Now that the Dark Lord had taken over the castle it

made things worse. Before, King Toby had used the castle and maze for the townsfolk to pick fruit and vegetables, but only as much as they needed. Now the Dark Lord used it as a punishment. He would send them into the depths of the maze to wander aimlessly around, not knowing where to go next, and to make things worse, many deadly plants now grew there. In short, the townsfolk lived in fear and dread, for now the Dark Lord ruled the magical country of Rhyce.

All except one group of rebels. They were called the Troopers, because they marched up and down the streets, protesting. They came from all different races: the Trogs, a sturdy ogre-like bunch; the Fuzz, a furry race who loved to be free; the Splods, who were just arms, legs and head; the Freewheelers, who had no legs, but instead used a small wheel; and the Humans, who used weapons and destroyed nature, until the year 2000, when the world was totally ruined and some came to live on the planet Rhyce.

All these races had joined forces to rise up against the Dark Lord. But some had become his slaves, fearing him because of what he might do to them if they were found out.

One young Splod's mother and father had been thrown into the maze, which made him even more angry. Another older Fuzz had had his farm terrorized by the sweepers, huge metal monsters, servants of the Dark Lord who would usually dwell around the castle, waiting for an order to destroy.

Now that the Troopers had started to rise up the Dark Lord became angry and sent goblins round to keep the peace.

Meanwhile, back in the Great Hall the Dark Lord sat wondering, and as he wondered he stared up at the rafters holding the roof up – but not any more! He muttered some strange words under his breath and two beams were transformed into strange dragon-like creatures. They swooped down and out of the huge wooden doors and then glided elegantly down the valley to the village of the rebels.

The village was empty of normal townsfolk for only the rebels dared to stay there. The dragons flew down alleyways looking, staring, and then suddenly a shout pierced the silence. It was a Trog, shrieking from the narrow door of a circular house. The dragons turned, bewildered. There was a patter of feet and then a huge roaring sound as thousands of rebels come thundering down the dirt track.

Dust swirled around them and the whole world of rebels and dragons was caught in a cloud of dust for one second. But as soon as the dust cleared, one dragon dropped like a dart and collected its prey – a Trog – then flew back up the valley to the forbidden castle.

The Dark Lord stared longingly out of the lancet window, awaiting the arrival of the two dragons and what prisoners they might have. As they came in sight he slammed down his silver goblet and cried, 'One measly Trog!' He had expected more from two dragons, but no. 'My servants will bring me what I want!' he cried.

Back in the village the rebels were plotting. 'We must do something. That is the third rebel to have been seized by the evil claws of the Dark Lord,' shouted an old Splod.

'I agree. I have some weapons in my hut,' said a Human gleefully.

'No! We shall not use your type of weapons. You used weapons and look at your planet now,' a frustrated Splod spluttered out.

There was a big hullabaloo and people started fighting and shouting because they disagreed with each other's plans, until a short, stout little man with no legs and just a wheel arrived. He was like a Freewheeler but slightly different. He had just appeared from nowhere, as if someone had planted instant-grow seeds on that exact spot. He was carrying a large crystal ball, a big jar full of green mixture medicines, saucepans and many other things in one rucksack.

'Hello,' a young, clear, crisp voice bellowed out, but quietened as he drew their attention. 'I'm Jab, half-man, half-bike – I keep running myself over. Yesterday I was looking into my crystal ball and saw you chasing those dragons down the valley, and the way you looked gave me the impression you needed some help, so here I am!'

'Ah! So the Freewheeler Jab has joined forces with the Troopers. Idiotic, insolent little beast. His magic and willpower will strengthen them. They might defeat me! Defeat me! But I will show them. I will show them!' screamed the Dark Lord.

Meanwhile, back in the village, Jab was showing some of the older Troopers a plan he had devised on his way through the valley.

'I say we go up the valley on sluzback, so then we are not worn out when we arrive at the castle.'

'Yes, but how do we get 150 or so sluz?' said a Splod.

'We don't, but we get seven or eight people trained and ready,' answered Jab.

'How will we know who to send?' asked an inquisitive Freewheeler.

'I have already thought of that,' said Jab. 'We will have some tests.'

So the testing began. It involved magic, chemistry and skill.

Eight Troopers were chosen from their marks in the tests. There was one Splod, Caz, a young, bright magician; one Freewheeler, Pop, a speedy, skilled young warrior; three Trogs, all sluzback riders; two of the Fuzz, Zag, who loved chemistry, and Ozrey, who knew every spell to know; a wise old Fuzz; and a Human called Damian, a clever, bright spark. Of course Jab was at the front.

'Right,' said Jab, 'Pop, you go now and get us some sluz.'

As soon as he had spoken, Pop was wheeling his way to the sluz fields.

No more than an hour passed, and Pop and some sluz were entering the town, one behind another like goslings following their mother. But an old woman hobbled out and cried, 'They've all gone to the old barn', cackled and walked away. Pop sped through the village to the old barn and cried, 'Come, we must go now while we can!' So the brave group started the long trek to the forbidden castle.

As they came to a small wood the Dark Lord looked down on them from the roof of the South Tower. 'Ah, so they have come this far already. Well, let's slow them down a bit.' He chuckled, to the delight of some goblins behind him, and threw a blue spark of light towards the trees. It hit one tree and where the tree had been, now stood three giant trolls.

They stood tall and straight, with one eye placed precisely in the middle of the head. One turned and threw a boulder at Jab. His sluz bolted, but Jab held on and when his sluz had calmed down he threw a bottle of brown mixture at the troll. Its contents sprayed all three trolls and soon they had become stone.

'They have eluded me yet again' yelled the Dark Lord, 'but no more. My pet worms will show them the way back to the village.' And with that he walked up the stairs to the North Tower.

Pop had stopped for a drink and was sitting on a rock when suddenly, 'Roar!' – a huge black worm writhed out and swallowed Pop's sluz. Then two more squirmed out. Dirt and mud was flying and everything was in a whirl, but a small blue crystal shot into one worm's mouth and it shrivelled up into nothing, and soon the same fate would occur to the other two.

'Who did that?' cried Damian. 'I did!' said a small voice. 'I'm Spluz, small and meek, an orphan but adopted by the Podlings and taught about the blue crystal. That's how I saved you.'

'But who are the Podlings? I have never heard of them,' said Jab.

In quick reply Spluz said, 'Well, hundreds of years ago the blue crystal was shattered. Many races found a shard of the blue crystal and moved to make their own territory – some above ground, some below. The Podlings chose to live below. The Dark Lord found the largest crystal shard and so has most power, but now let us go below.'

He said some mystical words and on a marshy patch two clumps of grass opened to reveal a flight of stairs. It was very murky and damp down below and there were many strange noises.

'It's creepy down here,' said Jab.

Then they heard strange music coming from a wooden door.

'That is the entrance to the forbidden castle,' said Spluz, 'and it is where I must leave you. So, goodbye,' and with that Spluz was gone.

'Come on. Let's go,' said Nebug, eldest of the Trogs, and slammed through the door. On the other side hundreds of goblins charged at them. Watching, the Dark Lord sat rubbing his hands together. He then raised one arm and held it aloft to the rebels and goblins. His hand became red, sparks starting to fly, and whatever he touched became stone.

Only three Troopers were immobilized, but Caz could not move; he was held by some magic. Still Pop, Jab and Damian went on, with Ozrey, but not for long! Ozrey fell down the moat and drowned, and Pop was speared by a small goblin. Jab confronted the Dark Lord for the key to the casket of light and died in the task.

But now Damian had the key and he opened the casket and the castle was flooded with light. The Dark Lord fell to his knees and cried, 'I'm ruined . . . ruined . . . ruined.' His voice became a whisper and he and his servants became dust. Damian opened all the windows and doors. The light poured in and once again Rhyce was filled with LIGHT.

The Message of the Watch

Kate Bryan

The solemn face stared up at me. Two slim arms lay outstretched under the scratched glass. Attached to the face was a thin, black strap. It had come to me, this old, yet dainty watch, from my mother for my birthday. After that day when I received it, strange things began to happen. I let the watch slither through my fingers for several minutes, recalling the happenings it had taken me through.

I remember it all started when I was fidgeting with the watch in bed on the night of my birthday. Disappointment swept over me as I realized that the watch wasn't working and still showed the time that I had first set the hands to. I felt like bursting into tears. Again and again I turned the watch over, in frustration, tapping the face but it was no good – it just didn't work.

At that moment I noticed some engravings on the back of the face. I held the watch steadily under my bedside light, tilting it from side to side. It read:

Never to be sold.
Never to be moved from this place.
Never to be destroyed.

Sold . . . moved . . . destroyed . . . NEVER. Why ever not? I pondered deeply over these words. Were they some kind of warning? Was the watch trying to tell me something? No, how silly! My imagination was getting the better of me again!

As I leaned over to switch off the light, the face seemed almost human, hypnotizing. Forcing my eyes away from its gaze, I quickly switched off the light.

As usual the room was dark and still, but I was conscious of a tiny dim light gleaming through the shadow-cast room. Turning towards it, I discovered that it was that irritating face glowing a luminous green!

With exasperation I buried myself deeply under my pillow and, breathing a sigh of relief, I settled down to sleep. In the silence came a pleading: TING-TING-TING . . .

'This is just too much.'

I flung back the pillow, having already decided to dispose of this useless gift, but there, lying quietly on the mattress, was an innocent little face looking up at me.

'What's your game, little one?' I whispered.

'TING-TING,' came an excited reply as the fingers whirled speedily past the numbers and then gradually ground to a halt. I stared at the watch until my eyes grew heavy and I drifted into a deep sleep.

Next morning I woke to the sun streaming through my window. The whole of Saturday lay ahead. In an instant my thoughts switched back to the night before. I was encouraged to get dressed quickly and, without hesitation, put on the watch. The sun welcomed me as I burst out of the house and skipped to the gate. As I opened the gate the familiar 'TING' rang out again, persuading me to look at the face.

To my amazement the hands slowly arranged themselves until they were both pointing to the number nine.

'Oh, mischievous one,' I said boldly, 'you've totally baffled me. What am I to make of this?'

Then an idea flashed into my head. The fingers were pointing to the *direction* and not the time.

'Nine means left', and so I set off, taking large, springy steps. 'This is the real test,' I murmured with a beaming smile. The crossroads lay ahead! Stopping abruptly at the crossroads, I listened intently. There was a faint 'TING', almost drowned by the roaring of the traffic. The fingers were pointing quite clearly to the three. 'Three means right,' I thought to myself, and proudly strode in that direction, down the lane.

To my surprise, some minutes later the watch tinged again and pointed left, but this time there was only a hedge. I carefully studied the hedgerow of dense, thick leaves. I peered through the hedge, feeling rather conspicuous and hoping that there were no passers-by. Through a gap I spotted a narrow, muddy track leading into the forest beyond. I scrambled eagerly through the hole, barely noticing the spiky branches which brushed against me. After following the track, the thick, dark, gloomy woods confronted me. I stared ahead into the darkness, then back at the easy way out through the gap in the hedge.

A sorrowful 'TING' drew me like a magnet into the forest and in no time at all I felt soft, crunching leaves and twigs crackling beneath my feet.

Sunlight peeped through the bright-green leaves sending shadowy patterns on to the ground. Birds twittered contentedly and a friendly atmosphere prevented me from being scared.

Above the general buzz there came a sharp, excited 'TING'. Then another and another. Faster and faster the hands began to whirl around the face until it was impossible to see them. I stopped and looked around. Just behind the bushes my attention was drawn to a glint of light reflecting on a shiny surface. Bubbling with excitement, I burst through the overgrown mass of leaves which parted to reveal an old wooden hut with just one open window and a neat little arched door.

'TING-TING-TING,' cried the watch.

'Be patient!' I exclaimed, even though I was feeling just as excited. I moved cautiously towards the door and gently pushed. The door groaned a little, then unexpectedly flew open! I tumbled in. The floor was coated with dust and shavings of wood. Before I had time to pull myself together I was aware of faces looking down at me.

These were no ordinary faces but were the round and lonesome faces of . . . CLOCKS! What a sorrowful sight. Four proud and motionless clocks, carved so carefully and shaped so beautifully. This was a real adventure!

I stepped towards the Grandfather clock in the corner and on its case the familiar words were engraved:

Never to be sold.
Never to be moved from this place.
Never to be destroyed.

Turning to the watch I muttered, 'This wasn't a game after all.'

The watch was silent for a change, which said everything. I studied the Grandfather clock carefully and noticed a large winding key. My fingers couldn't resist turning the key until it wouldn't wind any more.

A deep, hollow and solemn voice boomed, 'Thank you.'

This remark left me in a state of shock. It was incredible.

'Don't be afraid, little girl,' the voice continued. 'You have done us a great favour.' He glanced down at my wrist watch with a smile.

I looked up at his round and silvery-tinted face, with the black Roman numerals circling the rim, and the hollow voice came again from inside the case.

'Many, many years ago, when your Grandad was a boy, this shed was my master's workshop. We four clocks and our friend the watch were made skilfully by his nimble fingers. As we were so special, our master devoted most of his time to us and he treasured us dearly. He seemed to spend much more time on my wooden case and I've got something inside me which enables me to talk and understand humans.

'Each day my master came at the same hour to wind and polish us, and I was good friends with him. One day he did not come at that time. A day passed and there was still no sign of him. The time went very slowly as my mind was telling me that perhaps he had died. This would mean the end of us too, unless we acted quickly before we wound down to our doom. We all agreed that the watch was our only hope of getting a message through to someone who would help us.

'Plans were made for the watch to leave and the cuckoo clock helped to push him through the open window, where he fell outside in the undergrowth. We must have stood here for years after that terrible day until, not long ago, we spotted a lady putting the watch into her basket and disappearing out of the woods.'

'That must have been my mother, as she gave the watch to me for my birthday. Don't worry. I will come in replacement of your master to wind and polish you all.'

There was a chorus of 'TINGS' and 'CUCKOOS' following this remark.

This is what I did in secret for about a year, until on one visit, to my horror, the bulldozers were toppling the trees near the clocks' home. I panicked for the lives of my friends and ran desperately to the lorry driver. It took lots of breathless explaining to make him understand, but when he did, he gave a hearty laugh and agreed to transport the clocks on his lorry to my house.

The four clocks now live in my bedroom and I cherish them as their master did. It was only a week ago when walking to school with my friend that she asked inquisitively, 'Why ever don't you get rid of that silly old watch? I mean, it doesn't even tell the time.'

I glanced down at the watch, sharing a secret.

'Me? . . . Get rid of this watch . . . NEVER!'

A Day in the Life
of a Spider

Claire Brotherton

Another day is starting.

'Yawn.'

Well, time to get up and ready. Well, breakfast will be served in a minute.

Ahh! Breakfast, that was delicious. Now for the big business.

Oh no, arrrh!

My, that was close!

I'll hurry up and get into the box place. Any minute now that person will get that piece of paper and wack me with it! I don't know why I bother, but a spider's got to do what a spider's got to do!

I've got past those sliding doors. Well, here they come.

While I was thinking of all this, there was a strange and loud buzzing noise. I didn't bother looking round. I ran up the nearest wall! It was the giant people and they had a new friend who was buzzing angrily. They called him vacuum cleaner, so before standing for any more I scurried away.

Later on that day, after being nearly washed down the plughole, I went past vacuum cleaner.

'Goodnight,' I said.

He gave a 'buzz' quite happily.

When I got home I felt quite happy. I had made a new friend, but I wonder what language he speaks?

The Cricketers from Mars

David Main

One day in Oxford, Granny took me to the University Parks to watch a cricket match. The batsmen were in good form and sixes started to fly. One went heading for the chestnut trees close beside us. I ran to retrieve the ball and as I threw it back to a fielder I noticed something unusual in the long grass and heard a sound like a robot talking. I looked again. There was a saucer-like object in the grass beside me.

I picked it up curiously and a little red creature looked out. I jumped back in amazement and dropped the saucer-like object in doing so. Then I heard the little red creature say something like, 'Ouch!' I noticed some writing on the saucer. I think it said, 'Please return to Mars' and something else which I could not understand.

The little red creature said, 'Hello, my name is Zikro. What is your name and can I be your friend?'

I blinked my eyes in sheer bewilderment and could hardly believe my ears. Then I said, 'David is my name and of course I'll be your friend.'

'Oh, I am pleased,' replied the little red man, dancing about for joy.

I invited him over to meet Granny and to have something to eat from her basket. Granny sat there, her eyes popping out of her head as Zikro casually sat between us to watch the cricket as he nibbled a biscuit. All of a sudden another six was coming towards us and Zikro jumped up, catching the ball in his mouth.

The fielders were running across to us, thinking he was hurt, as all they could see was red – the colour of blood. Zikro laughed in his Martian way, saying, 'This is how we catch balls in Mars whenever we play cricket.'

The cricketers were astounded and just stood there completely dumb-struck. The *Sunday Times* cricket correspondent, who happened to be nearby, came across and introduced himself, hoping he would get a story.

'What about a cricket team from Mars? I can send a signal and they can be here in no time,' suggested Zikro.

The correspondent could see this would make headlines in his paper. Zikro sent the signal, which was just a whistle, and his team appeared from the long grass in no time, as he had said. By this time many spectators were gathered round us, all as curious as could be.

It was agreed to play a match there and then. The little red men with their little red cricket bats were invited to bat first, Zikro taking the first ball. He played it high into the sky and we all thought it was going to be a six, but a boundary fielder was there. It looked like a grand catch but, alas, the fielder dropped it. After that there was no stopping Zikro, and when Zunk was caught at the other end for forty-two, Zikro had reached his century. The spectators were delighted at such lovely cricket. In two hours time Zikro's team were all out for 409 runs.

Then it was their turn to bowl to the Oxford team. Runs came slowly as Oxford were very cautious, but they could not hold out for ever and were all out for 190 runs because the bowling and fielding were so good. Zikro's team being clear winners, they had a great handclap from the crowd – more spectators having arrived during play.

The little red men quietly slipped into the long grass again. Zikro said goodbye to me and to the Oxford players. He said that they must be off as they had an important match against Jupiter the next day. He also asked if they could come again, and the Oxford players and I arranged to meet them by the Rainbow Bridge on the same date next year.

Their large spacecraft was perched on the chestnut tree branches, and one by one they climbed up into it in their saucer-like spacesuits. Next morning the *Sunday Times* had the match report on their front page, with pictures covering all the match. Later on, the reporter won the prize for the best cricket story of the year.

The Stranger

Jacob Nevins

In 2974 a cataclysmic explosion in New York marked the start of the Great Atomic War. It was the most devastating war mankind had ever known. Energy shields gave way before the great T-bomb, made from a new and deadly element called Thorite, whose nuclei were fused together using an H-bomb. One T-bomb could lay waste 1,000 square kilometres.

In 3071 American refugees found out how to power engines with antimatter. They built crude starships and escaped to outer space. The refugees forgot Earth. From these first explorers the great Galactic Empire grew up.

Dr Aubrey Simms was at the Nuclear Research Center, Chicago, on 15 January 1988. He was making an electrolytic aluminium determination. Suddenly he noticed a blue corona over the platinum crucible. What? This was only crude uranium! How could fission be taking place?

Simms snatched up a metre-stick and knocked the lethal crucible to the ground. Metal thinly spattered the floor. Instinctively, he glanced around the room and noticed a tiny patch of daylight. It was coming from a small hole, about a centimetre wide, in the wall. Simms had never seen that before.

A beam travelling in a straight line, would expand and weaken, catching everything in its way.

He did not tell anyone about that belief.

He did not tell anyone that he got the papers next morning and hunted through them with a solid purpose. It was obvious from his fruitless search that nobody had run screeching to the police, with hysterical narratives about a man (or part of a man) disappearing in front of their eyes.

Howard Deboe was strolling outside the Nuclear Research Center on the same day. He bent down to pick up a coin. He had a momentary dizzy sensation and, straightening up, he saw a glowing wood. Here and there were cracked paving-stones and a few bricks. Most of the trees were just leafless hulks. No grass grew. To his left there was a great clearing. The glowing was more intense there, like a thousand fireflies.

Deboe fainted.

Captain Hecto T. Stannack frowned. It had been three days since they had crash-landed on this radioactive planet. Three days since Engineer Zebedee Grova had burst on to the bridge, saying that the hyperdrive had failed. Seven people had died, and the crash had rendered the crew's quarters uninhabitable.

Exactly how the hyperdrive had failed was not certain. It was Grova's view that a diode had blown in the ultrasonic wave system, while others thought that the antimatter stockpile had run out.

*

When Deboe came to, he could not think what had happened to him. It was dark, and the stars were coming out. There was a light breeze blowing with a metallic tang to it.

Deboe got up and ran. He ran and ran, groping wildly in the darkness. He ran until he stumbled on a root and collapsed, gasping, on the hard ground.

When the research party returned, Zee Prime reported to the captain that the planet which they had landed on was W-243 in the Sol Sector, 3 parsecs away from their original destination. There had been no signs of life on the planet.

Grova had said that the hyperdrive could be mended but that it would take several weeks. He was partly right, because it was found that ever since they had passed through that magnetic storm, a diode had been working loose in board 214.

Deboe had come to the conclusion that either he had gone mad or something very strange had happened. The night had passed, and the thin mists of morning were wisping between the stumps. The first thought that came to his mind when he awoke was that he was hungry. He searched around, hunting for something to eat. While he was looking, he came across a giant clearing. He saw a huge metallic disc, bigger than the Colosseum. The front part seemed to be crushed badly. Dotted all around it were whitish dome-shaped things.

Deboe fled, his mind refusing to acknowledge what he had seen.

Stannack jumped. Was that the last thing he expected on this planet, another human being? It seemed to have sprung out from behind a tree, and then jumped and crouched down. He summoned Prime.

'Are you sure there isn't any life on this planet?'

'Positive, sir.'

'Well, send out your research party to that section of the woods, because I think that there's a man there.' He pointed.

'Are you sure, sir? The radioactivity on this planet is high enough for life not to have evolved!'

'Get on with it!'

Sullenly, Prime walked away and called his colleagues.

Deboe, desperate for food, decided to return to where he had seen the disc. He was now positive as to what it was.

His earlier hunt for food had been unsuccessful. All he had found was a stunted bush bearing some shrivelled nuts. However, while he was searching, he found a burnt sign saying:

> STITUT
> FOR
> UCLEA
> SEARC

He remembered that he had been walking outside the Nuclear Research Center before it all changed.

Suddenly he noticed men coming out of one of the domes. They wore bulky-looking clothes, as if they were wearing lots of padding. The men spotted Deboe, and came running towards him. They quietly surrounded him and closed in. One of them drew out a slim, black cylinder from his pocket.

The last thing that Deboe remembered was a flash of light.

Stannack was amazed. How could someone be living out there without a radiation suit? The analysis showed that his clothes were made of thin cellulose. There were some copper-nickel discs and rectangular pieces of paper in a mammal-skin wallet.

Medical examination showed that the man was about forty. He had thirty-two teeth and greyish hair. That was impossible! The maximum nowadays was sixteen teeth, and people had usually balded at about twenty. It all seemed to say that he was a living fossil from the mythical pre-Galactic Era.

The radiation count of his bones showed that he could not have been on this planet for more than four days. But he couldn't have just appeared here, so what had happened?

Inside the spaceship, Deboe was rather surprised. What he had expected to see were flashing red and white lights, gleaming control panels and rows of high-tech visiscreens. What he saw was a normalish-looking room with fluorescent tubes for lighting. The only odd thing about it was the glistening silver equipment in the far corner.

Deboe had decided that, somehow, he must have travelled forward in time. He had no idea how. The Third World War must have happened while he was away! All those centuries of technological build-up, just to disappear in a nuclear holocaust. All that hope: space station by 2015, base on Mars by 2020, Alpha Centauri by 2095! All gone! Bang! The human race wiped out in an ominous mushroom cloud.

Where, then, had this saucer in the sky come from? Betelgeuse? Mars? He could not guess. And why did the aliens look so human?

Stranger and stranger. All this strange man would utter were low moans, hisses and clicks. The odd thing was, though, that the sounds were almost exactly the same as 6,700-year-old audiotapes found on a planet orbiting Altair. All these reports seemed to say that he had time-travelled from the past.

Repair on the hyperdrive had gone much more quickly than he had expected. By tomorrow they would be ready to go. There was hot debate about whether they should continue on to their destination or go back to Sirius.

Deboe felt a roaring in his ears and a humming in the room. The ship must be taking off, he thought. He wondered what sort of transgalactic spacedrive equipment it used.

Later one of the men came in and gave him a plastic bowl of something. It had a shiny film over the top and was cold, but when the man pressed something it warmed up and the cover peeled off. It was a type of soup with chunks of something in it. Deboe liked it, but it had a very slight metallic tang.

They had managed to get off that wretched radioactive dirtball at last! Joyously, the ship passed by its natural satellite, Luna, and out of W-243's orbit. It passed Sol by, and zoomed out of the sector, headed for Sirius.

Stannack had an idea. The psychophone! He told Prime and all the others about it. They rushed to the locker it was kept in and hastily unlocked it. Then they ran to the strange man's room and plugged the psychophone in to one of the electroterminals. Stannack switched on. The liquid gibberish that came out of the man's mouth suddenly settled down to Galactic Standard.

Deboe heard English words and saw pictures of gleaming cities, star-studded space, exotic landscapes. He learned about spaceships, about Galactic history, about the universe.

And he and the ship hurtled on, to a destiny he could not guess.

Inspector Green

Haggai Scolnicov

Police Surgeon Emdee (MD, Cantab.) walked into the hallway of Number 46, Street 12, Sector G. Inspector Green looked up.

'Dead?' he asked.

The surgeon's head nodded slowly. 'Knocked down and throttled. Probably dead for two or three hours before we came.'

Green stood up slowly and entered the bedroom. Miss Bentley's body lay on the floor, her head lolling sideways. The Inspector was not troubled. He was not a sentimental man – indeed, he wasn't a man at all. He was a robot, designed to investigate police cases. His sleek, cylindrical body was covered by a layer of springy foam (green, as his name implied) and his various arms were fitted with the newest types of robot police tools.

Carefully he inspected the area by the dead woman for clues. A metal detector on arm 5 called his attention to something on the floor. A light magnetic current separated some grains from the dust on the floor. He brought them close to one of his many eyes, and inspected them at a magnification of 250 times. It was rust, he thought, not a common thing to find in a world using plastics and high-resilience metallic alloys.

'Emdee,' he called. 'Could you tell me what type of rust this is?'

Emdee came in and took the rust grains silently. A door in his body slid open and he placed the rust inside carefully. The door closed and reopened after some time, a smaller amount of rust being revealed. 'I detect iron, I think,' said Emdee. 'Probably steel.'

Nothing suggestive there, thought Green, but where could Miss Bentley find steel? Who used steel nowadays?

He searched carefully but found nothing else. Twenty minutes later, he was finishing his report to Chief Inspector Bradley, his human overseer.

'So you see, sir, there are no clues at the scene except the body and the steel rust.'

'Yes,' said Bradley, 'I see.' He appeared to be pondering the matter. 'And what will you do next?' he inquired.

'Well, I was thinking about questioning Mr Robert Crane, the man who found the body.'

Bradley frowned. 'He's already been questioned. He doesn't know a thing. Still, if you think it would be beneficial . . .'

Inspector Green knocked twice on the door. It opened after some time and a robot shuffled forward. The domestic machine gazed rather stupidly at the Inspector.

'Good morning,' said Green. 'I'm Green.'

The robot accepted this statement gravely and

inspected the Inspector's emerald covering. Its small head nodded in agreement.

'Perhaps I didn't make myself clear enough. I am Inspector Green from the police. I phoned earlier. May I come in?'

'Of course, Inspector,' came the reply. 'So good of you to come. Robert hasn't been the same since Miss Bentley died. She'd been his secretary for fourteen years now, you know.' The mechanical butler turned and showed Green into a small room.

A tall, brown-haired man was finishing his lunch. He stood up. 'Inspector Green, excuse me. I'll be ready in a moment.' He typed something on a small keyboard and the table disappeared into the wall. 'I expect you want to question me about . . . Ah . . .' His voice trailed off.

'No, I don't. Obviously you've been quite upset.'

'Yes, I didn't . . . I mean, it wasn't . . .' His voice broke again.

'I understand, Mr Crane. I realize that humans feel these emotions.'

Robert Crane sat there quietly. He didn't move, he didn't speak. He just sat, lost in thought.

There was something, thought Green, a bit odd. Something wrong, artificial, overdone. When had he first noticed? The robot at the door . . . something he had said . . . what was it? He began replaying the short conversation. Before he had gone through much, though, his chain of thought was broken by Mr Crane.

'So, what did you want to know, Inspector?'

'I wanted to know some details about your work. You are in . . .?'

'Law. I'm legal adviser at Archer Domestic Robots Co.'

'I see.' Green thought he almost realized something important. He needed time.

'Your butler is an Archer BX 5 704, isn't it?'

Crane started slightly, then tried to conceal the fact. 'Yes, I think he is.' He looked nervous. 'Shiny but not very bright.' He laughed shrilly at his joke, then quietened.

Now Green was practically sure. He radioed Sarge, the central police computer, and asked for three robots: two of the small 'Rovers' and a PC Plod.

'Do you have a hobby, Mr Crane?'

'No. Well, yes, if you count ancient weapons.'

'You mean swords and guns, that stuff?'

'Yes. I could show you my collection.'

They entered a small room, crammed with shelves containing old weapons of every description. Green was fascinated. His wide reading while training as a detective enabled him to identify many of the weapons. He had not, however, seen the actual objects before.

Crane showed the Inspector around the room, explaining the usage of each weapon. A small table in the far corner caught Green's attention. He started towards it.

'And what are these?' he inquired.

'Those! Oh, they're just old pistols,' he said, with a distinct lack of interest. 'Twin-barrelled things, you know, two shots.'

'Fascinating, such workmanship, such . . .'

He didn't finish the sentence. He'd just noticed that one of the pistols had less dust on it than the others. Had it been used recently? Could the rust at the scene of the crime be from this pistol? Had Crane perhaps shot at Miss Bentley and missed, then strangled her. Or had . . . had the mechanical manservant killed Miss Bentley on Crane's orders? Unknown to Crane, Green was at this moment flashing a message to Sarge: 'Investigate, victim's room, by desk, two lead pellets, approx. 12 mm across.'

He followed Crane out of the room. Green knew that, under the three Laws of Robotics (attributed to Mr Asimov, twentieth-century visionary), no robot would kill a human being, or cause harm to one. If, however, it believed that the death of a person was necessary to ensure the safety of others, it might kill. Had Crane convinced his robot that Miss Bentley must die? In the cause of justice he must find out. He had a plan . . .

'I suppose you've also picked up some robotics at your job, Mr Crane?'

'Well . . . I . . .'

'Enough,' continued Green, 'to know that a robot would kill a human being if it was convinced that this was the only way to save many human lives?'

'I don't know what you mean!' Robert Crane shouted.

'Enough, perhaps, to realize that you could convince your BX 5 704 that he must murder Miss Bentley?'

While Crane spluttered with rage, Green received his confirmation from Sarge: 'Rover 2714 found objects as described. Important note: suspect owed money to victim.'

'Better save your explanations for the judge,' said Green. 'We've found the bullets,' he explained.

Crane quietened. He stared in front of him at a point in the middle of nowhere. Green began his temporary arrest.

'As a robot in the service of the police I place you, Robert Crane, ID number 953/TL/071, under temporary arrest by the authority given to me under Clause C of the Robotic Police Assistants Act. You will be escorted to the nearest police station, where you will be handed over to a human police employee. If you have any queries as to your rights or any other points of law, I will be glad to print or read out to you the law or laws concerned. I may also explain the mentioned information in a limited fashion. Do you wish to inform someone of your temporary arrest?'

Crane shook his head slowly.

Green heard the police robots entering and turned to take Crane's arm.

'Please come with me.'

Concerned, the sobbing man whipped out a hidden pistol from his collection. He shot at the Inspector but missed, the bullet spraying rust as it flew. The second shot misfired and wounded Crane's own arm. The robots had now entered and Green told them to carry the wounded man to a hospital.

A satisfactory case, all in all, reflected Green. A typical example of the 'butler dunnit' murder. All the facts fitted wonderfully, you just had to find the pattern behind them. First the robot at the door. 'Good of you to come,' he'd said. This wasn't true. For a simple robot like that 'good' meant helpful at their job. Police were not 'good'. In effect, only one thing would cause a robot to lie to a policeman (or police robot) when it had been programmed not to. That thing was the possibility of causing harm to a human. The robot was obviously shielding its master and itself, murderer by its master's decree. Crane, too, had been nervous and ill at ease, especially after the robot was mentioned. Seeing the rusty pistol was pure luck, and the rest was just an educated guess, even though he himself had been pretty certain. A pity nothing could be done about the homicidal robot. Or maybe . . . ?

Ten minutes later, Green stood in the room where the BX 5 704 had hidden. Broken furniture was strewn across the floor and the battered remains of the robotic butler lay in one corner of the room. Green had just finished arresting himself for '. . . wilful destruction of the property of one Mr Robert

Crane, including a robotic machine' and had noted the offender's claim to lack of credit to pay the fine. His sense of justice satisfied, he left the house and began the long walk back to the station.

The Adventures of
Firfrizzle and Caterdragon

Roger Cox

CHAPTER 1: BATBRAIN

Once upon a time there were two monsters called Firfrizzle and Caterdragon. One day they had a baby called Rabder, who looked like a spider with rabbit's ears. Soon after Rabder was born, they met a monster called Batbrain. Batbrain was a friendly monster, so Firfrizzle and Caterdragon invited him home for tea. On the way home, a mond carried off Rabder. Monds were bird-like monsters with fangs in their beaks and spikes in their tails.

CHAPTER 2: CAPTURE

Firfrizzle said, 'We won't have time to have tea. Will you help us rescue Rabder?'

'OK,' said Batbrain.

Meanwhile, the mond was flying over a mountain with a cave in it. A slyskinner came out and snarled. The mond looked scared and fluttered up, screaming, and landed on a tree that the slyskinner couldn't climb.

Firfrizzle, Caterdragon and Batbrain had just recovered from the total shock of the mond and Batbrain flew to find the mond. Soon he found the tree and attacked the mond, which interested the slyskinner, who put twigs and bracken round and set fire to it by rubbing sticks together. At that instant Caterdragon leapt out of the undergrowth and killed the slyskinner. The mond flew away in total panic and so did Batbrain, carrying Rabder. When they got home a pinchpoker stopped them from getting in and started pinching and poking them. Caterdragon immediately attacked and soon a fearsome battle was afoot.

CHAPTER 3: THE PINCHPOKER

Caterdragon was winning the battle and the pinchpoker was at his mercy. Just then, Caterdragon heard Firfrizzle shriek. So he tied the pinchpoker up and ran to help. Soon he got there and asked who Firfrizzle was leaning over.

Firfrizzle said, 'I made friends with this monster. He is called Trickcheek.'

At that moment the pinchpoker yelled, 'I can help you! Trickcheek has been poisoned and I can help you by telling you what the antidote is and where it is. You cross the river which is guarded by the monorm. You go through the forest with the traps of the ancient monsters and finally arrive by the pit of Charclonius, the ancient monster-killer. Inside the pit is the fireplant, which is the antidote. The fireplant has only two petals. At night it is ablaze with fire but it never gets burnt. Only human hands can pick the flower without catching fire. After the flower is picked, Trickcheek must eat it to be brought back to life.'

Caterdragon untied the pinchpoker, who ran off before they could ask any questions.

CHAPTER 4: THE RIVER OF THE MONORM

Firfrizzle and Rabder went home and Caterdragon and Batbrain went on the quest of the fireplant. Soon they found the river of the monorm, so Batbrain flew along and Caterdragon clung on. When they were nearly there a serpent-like monster towered above them. They recognized it immediately as a monorm. Batbrain flew up but the monorm jumped to the same height as Batbrain, so he swooped to the side and landed at the other side of the river.

CHAPTER 5: THE FOREST WITH THE TRAPS OF THE ANCIENT MONSTERS

Where they had landed was the edge of a dark, ghostly wood. As soon as they landed a net fell and a furry bright-eyed demon came walking towards them. Caterdragon used his spikes as marlinspikes to undo the knots, climbed on to Batbrain and they flew off. Soon they got to the other end of the wood, so they swooped down, but when they went between two branches in a V shape they snapped together and nearly broke Batbrain's wing joints. Caterdragon spiked his spikes at them but this merely made it more difficult to get out, because he got stuck. The last of the ancient monsters, a messenger monster, sent off an SOS call. It took him ages to find someone who believed him, but the only person in the land of monsters was Firfrizzle, so after many an adventure he arrived at the end of the forest with the traps of the ancient monsters, and bent the branches apart so that Caterdragon and Batbrain could fly off. They swooped down into the pit of Charclonius.

CHAPTER 6: THE SEARCH FOR A HUMAN

When they remembered that only human hands could touch the fireplant, Batbrain zoomed off and Caterdragon guarded the fireplant. As he flew along, Batbrain wondered how he could find a small human being that was light enough for him to carry. He flew out of the crater which was the doorway from Monsterland to the Pacific Ocean and headed towards England. He saw a very small car coming down the road. It had a funny sort of flag thing on it and there was some kind of beam coming out of it, so he followed it and nearly bumped into a human being.

He said, 'Hop on to my back, and I'll take you to monster country, where we have a crisis. One of us has been killed by poison and only human beings can pick the cure.'

'OK,' said Roger, and jumped on.

They soon arrived in monster country, at the pit of Charclonius.

CHAPTER 7: THE HOMEWARD JOURNEY

When they got to the Pit of Charlonius, they asked Roger to pick the fireplant. He picked it and they set off for home, Firfrizzle, Rabder and Trickcheek. As they saw the river of the monorm, they wanted to teach it a lesson, so they zoomed towards the river of the monorm, got stuck in a V trap and the monorm sprang and loosened them from the V trap! They flew off and landed back safely at home. They gave Trickcheek the antidote and Firfrizzle said, 'Why don't we go inside and have tea? Remember, we invited Batbrain round. Let's invite Trickcheek too.'

So they all had tea, and lived happily ever after.

The Computer Person

Polly Poynter

Alan sat at his work station, oblivious to the mess surrounding him. His bright-blue bedspread was crumpled and messy, distorting the aeroplanes and clouds on it. Model airships were lying scattered on the floor, along with floppy-disc covers and his screwed-up pyjamas. The curtains were half open, and Alan could see the beautiful view outside his window. He selected a floppy disc and inserted it into the Drive marked 'A'.

It whirred for five seconds. Alan frowned as he peered at the visual display unit. Instead of getting the spacegame 'Aliens', a message flashed at him: PLEASE*HELP*ME He pressed the space bar, hoping to clear it, and then the return key, to no avail. Finally, he switched off the power supply, but when he started it up again, the message was still there. Just for fun, he typed: OK*I'LL*HELP*WHAT*DO*YOU *WANT*ME*TO*DO? At once the message cleared and the game 'Aliens' appeared. Alan was thrilled when he beat them 9:0, but couldn't help feeling he had had some help.

The next day, when Alan rebooted the system, the strange message reappeared at the top of the screen. Again, he typed the sentence OK*I'LL*HELP*WHAT* DO*YOU*WANT*ME*TO*DO?, the screen responded

YOU*HAVE*TO****ML*LK*MMM . . . and his game appeared! This repetition annoyed Alan so much that he decided to take the communicator to the repair shop to get it looked at. Later that day, however, Alan realized he was short of pocket money, and took the back off the machine himself. When he got to the complex area of the 'brain', he found a tiny man, dressed in white overalls and wearing anti-static boots, trapped by a tiny drop of solder. The little man's chin was smoothly shaven, and his eyes were as blue as the sky on a summer's day. His hair was white and fluffed out around his head, and was so delicate that Alan could see every strand. His cheeks glowed like the embers of a dying fire and when he saw Alan, he smiled, his pink lips stretching to form dimples. He was certainly one of God's miracles!

'Hello,' he squeaked. 'So you are Alan.'

'Yes,' breathed Alan. 'But who are you?'

'I'm called Toxxix,' he replied, 'and I've been communicating with you through my capsule: your computer.'

'Yes, I gathered that much,' said Alan quietly, 'but what do you mean, "Help You"?'

Toxxix answered: 'Living in a capsule is awfully tiring. Just imagine, all those pieces of metal and plastic, twisting around and around, in and out, over and under. Anyway, when I was trying to communicate with you I had my foot stuck in a drop of solder.'

'But why did you need to contact me?' asked Alan, a little confused.

'That's what I've been trying to tell you,' said Toxxix, his voice dropping to a whisper. He looked around tentatively. 'I'm being hunted.'

Alan burst out laughing. 'Oh yeah. And my name's Bert Robinson!' However, he stopped laughing when he saw how serious the little man was.

'Not long ago, someone caught me,' said Toxxix, 'but they had no understanding. They tried to keep me prisoner, but I managed to escape.'

'Why did they want to keep you captive?' asked Alan.

'Because of my ability to enter the memory of any computer,' replied Toxxix. 'They wanted me to be a super-hacker. Will you help me?'

The little man clung to Alan's fingernail, pleading. It was an unbelievable story, but Alan was only ten and he trusted him. He made a decision.

'OK,' he replied. 'I'll help you, if I can. But I still don't understand how you managed to get into *my* computer.'

'It's a difficult thing for a person of your age to grasp. There was a massive negative transference from the 'Aliens' game you play with,' Toxxix explained. 'I have come from a universe on the other side of the ElectroCalculus and I can't get back!'

Alan considered carefully, then asked; 'Right. What do you want to eat?'

At the mention of food, saliva started to dribble down Toxxix's chin, his blue eyes shone and a crafty smile spread over his face. 'Food . . .' he sighed dreamily. 'My favourite. Cheeseburger ... hamburger ... ketchup ... peanut butter ... hotdogs ... cold chicken ... spamandcressrolls ... tomatocucumberandgarlicbreadwithlemonadeand ...'

'OK, OK,' interrupted Alan. 'Have a Rolo and like it. It's all I've got. There's some Coke in the fridge. I'll go and get it.' With that, he got up and went downstairs.

As soon as Alan left, Toxxix ran over to the window and slipped out. Being only 25 mm tall, he had no trouble working his way to the ground using the cracks and joints between the bricks to help. He ran across the road to the telephone box, where he illegally entered a code.

Liefrigge was there, waiting for the call.

'Well,' he asked, ''did you get it?'

Toxxix pulled from his pocket a minute tape recorder. 'Listen,' he whispered. 'I recorded it all.'

'Good,' replied Liefrigge, the master controller on Gruggrue 455. 'You've done a good job. You'll be recommended for a Medal Class One for this.'

Toxxix blushed at this unexpected praise. 'I must get back. Alan only went for some Coke.'

With that he slipped back across the road and re-entered the house. He was safely back on the windowsill when he called to Alan, 'I'm over here. What a view you have.'

Alan walked over, carrying the Coke. 'Yes. I wondered where you were. Would you like some chocolate?' He took a bar from his pocket and broke it. He looked at his watch. 'Is that the time! Mum and Dad will be back soon!' He threw off his clothes and put on his pyjamas while Toxxix ate his chocolate, then settled him into a large matchbox with a clean handkerchief for a duvet. 'Good night,' Alan whispered and squeezed the box shut.

Toxxix cursed. He had to get out. He threw off the handkerchief and, with his back on the floor he pushed on the top of the box with his feet. Slowly the box eased open and Toxxix, covered in sweat, slid out. He went over to the work station and searched for Alan's floppy discs to no avail. He returned to his matchbox and fell asleep.

He awoke the next day with a start. The matchbox that had become his home had blown on to the floor. Alan was already up and dressed and Toxxix soon brought the conversation round to Alan's computer discs.

'Yes,' said Alan, 'I realized you would want to see them, being the sort of person you are.'

For a moment Toxxix's heart stopped beating. Alan, seeing his horror-stricken face, said, 'You know so much about computers, it's natural.'

Toxxix gave a little laugh, his pulse returning to normal.

'I am glad I've found you!' Alan burst out. 'I have hardly any friends at school. All the other children call me Swot and I hate it. Just because I'm clever.'

Toxxix squirmed uncomfortably. He hated emotional scenes like these. He patted Alan's finger comfortingly and said, 'I'm your friend, Alan.'

Alan gave him a watery smile and said, 'Thanks, I know I can trust you.''

At this Toxxix went red and shuffled his feet. They both went over to the work station and Alan took some discs out of the drawer at the side. He selected one, and inserted it into the 'A' drive.

'Oh! Drat!' Alan explained. 'I forgot, I have to go to the village to do a paper round this morning. Cecil is on holiday. Will you be OK for an hour?'

Toxxix nodded agreement. This was too good too be true! As Alan went out, Toxxix got to work.

A:>submit*copy, he typed. The disc drive whirred and he copied the disc. He started to climb down to the floor when he slipped. He scrabbled to find a grip but banged his head on the desk and fell unconscious to the ground, blood trickling from a cut in his scalp.

Alan returned. 'Toxxix, where are you?' He searched, calling, to no avail. Perhaps he has gone back to his capsule, thought Alan, as he inserted 'Aliens' and booted the system.

At the top of the screen, a message: are*you*there?*

He trembled, then typed in the single word: yes.

my*name*is*zielief*i*am*a*protector*i*am* looking*for*a*traitor*named*toxxix*have* you*seen*him?*

yes, typed Alan, remembering the crafty smile. he *was*here**

The computer flashed again, but Alan was distracted. He felt something underfoot, something sticky, like chewing gum and wondered if he had trodden on some while delivering newspapers. Alan looked closely. It was certainly pinkish, but didn't look like gum. Then he noticed the white, fluffy hair, the overalls – now turned pink – and the small, crushed body of his so-called friend.

Runaway

Neil McRobert

John sat, huddled up in a ball, under a bush. It was raining in torrents and he flicked his eyes backwards and forwards through the trees, looking for someone who might report him for being in the park after hours.

John glanced wistfully across at the posh house, beautifully built, with a light-blue blind, laced with green, drawn across the window. He sighed and dragged his miserable suitcase of belongings into safety from the rain, which had formed a little puddle on the cracked, brown leather. He swept it off and opened it. Only half full, he thought, and cursed himself for running away so quickly.

'Should've waited a day or so,' John whispered hoarsely, gazing at his belongings, which included £102.75, a Walkman and a pair of jeans. There was no food. At least I won't get homesick, he thought, lying down on the soggy grass, clutching his suitcase.

It was 9.00 p.m. Four hours later he was awoken by a drunken shout.

'Oi, Basil!'

A swaying face, a foot from his own, was making a pouting, round-mouthed expression, as a child of three makes when it's found a wounded animal. He took a swig of cheap brandy and shouted again, 'Oi,

Basil.' The man's pronunciation was impeded, which made 'Basil' sound like 'Basiw'.

'Yesh?'

Another face, just as grotesque, poked in beside the first. He had a comical moustache, a brown toupee and carried a half bottle of Scotch. The new face spoke.

'Ish a ki . . . kiddywinkle,' he said, turning to his companion, who nodded solemnly. 'You a kiddywinkle?'

John, who was completely rigid with fear, managed to find his wits. 'Er, yes. Have you heard, they're giving away free spirits at the pub in Elm Tree Walk?'

'Hear that?' said the first face.

''Tis shoupa,' agreed the second. 'Bye bye, kiddywinkle. Shee you around.' And with that they staggered off through a hole in the hedge singing 'The one-eyed O'Riley'.

Recovering himself, John grabbed his suitcase, banging his shin with the strap. He cursed, and half hopped, half sprinted to the other side of the park, into the gardener's hut. He set his alarm for 6.00 a.m. and fell asleep for the second time that night.

John woke up the next morning wondering why it was so quiet, for once. Dad must be out, he thought, thank God. Then he remembered and clutched at his suitcase until the knuckles on his tanned hands became snowy white.

My God, he thought. I gottagetouta here. He

mumbled as he flung open the door. It was foggy, following the previous night's downpour. His leg still had an annoying ache as he hobbled up to the hole in the hedge where Basil and his companion had disappeared a few hours earlier. John wondered what the Elm Tree tenants thought of them and chuckled silently to himself as he limped through the damp morning air.

Food, he thought, staring at the pathetic logo of his local supermarket. He took £10 from his wallet, which he had taken from his case, and walked through the automatic doors. Walking through the store, John set his eyes on all the out-of-date stock, ate all the free samples he could find and went to the check-out desk.

'Doing the shopping for your mam, eh?' said the check-out girl, flashing John a smile. She turned to a colleague. 'Isn't that nice?' she said, still tapping on the keys with ringed fingers.

If only you knew, thought John, if only you knew.

Two weeks later a ragged, untidy youth emerged from the gents' toilet on the corner of the town precinct. The light-grey trainers which adorned his feet had turned dark with the soggy, damp weather. His T-shirt was muddy brown and his clenched fist held his last £10 note.

John scorned all shops that afternoon. His purposeful strides took him swiftly to the edge of town, and the arcades. He moved forward. For one moment his step seemed to falter.

No, he thought, you've gotta go. You've already risked. Ya gotta risk again.

He was inside. Not many people were in the arcade at this time of day, and that afternoon was no exception. A few punks were hanging around in the corner, swigging out of lager cans and laughing.

John took no notice and put his note in the change machine. A stream of ten-pence pieces came running out of the slot machine. In a sudden, unexplained memory John remembered the time when he had had a bad case of flu. He thought of the pain, the aches, while his parents went to a party.

'We'll be back in three or four hours,' John remembered his dressed-up mother saying. 'Don't be such a snivelling little baby.'

He had packed his bag that night. Ten days later, when he had recovered, he walked out of the door, vowing never to come back.

The clinking of the sterling in front of him returned his mind to the present. Gobbling up the coins greedily, John's eyes looked around the startling array of fruit machines that held the fantasies of many a teenager.

Not surprisingly, a system was something John had never bothered to learn. He walked up to the first fruit machine and stared at the mix of cherries, mangoes and grapefruit. Dipping into his pocket, he produced a coin and fondled it lovingly. As John pushed it into the slot, he raised his eyes in a silent prayer.

Bony fingers moved over the buttons as GAMBLE,

START, NUDGE and HOLD went down under the finger tips. A pound was put in. Twenty pence was taken out. Silver went through again and again. John looked at the machine that had avoided giving any money back to him.

He glared and moved on. He had noticed a punk watching the machine eagerly. As soon as John shuffled on, the punk, with a green Mohican, pounced and put in a coin. John turned back to watch him. One BAR, then two, and amazement hit John's eyes as a third stopped on the winning line.

Money poured out of the box above the shelf and clattered down into it. The punk grinned and scooped up the money that was so close to John.

'Unlucky, kid.' A ringed hand ruffled his hair and its owner walked off to another machine.

Slowly, sullenly, John shuffled out of the arcade and began to cry – drawn-out, hiccuping gulps that were almost silent. He wept, the tears blurring his brown eyes. John looked at the fifty pence piece in his hand. Suddenly he didn't care.

'One more try.'

The fifty pence entered the slot. Nothing came out.

Under the bush that night John made up his mind. He knew it was for the best. He'd lost everything, he knew that, and he needed a home, even a bad one. He fell asleep, his mind made up.

That morning, a sun as bright as a lighthouse bore through the bush. Hardly appropriate, John thought.

Almost ironic. He walked through the whole town, soaking up the sun, before coming to the street he used to live in.

He eyed his front door critically; the paint was chipped, the drainpipes rusting, with crumbling brickwork.

Shuddering, John took from his pocket the key that was never meant to be used, put it in the lock and turned it.

The Rabbit in the Moon

Dorianne Elliott

Mmutla, the wild hare, sat on a flat rock on the side of a kopje[1] and dozed, enjoying the warmth that still poured out from the rock. He peered up into the sky and marvelled at the full moon, slowly rising above the horizon and illuminating, with an eerie glow, the long grass and cruel thorns on the acacia trees. As he rose above the horizon, the rabbit in the moon seemed to be smiling down upon his earthly brother.

With only a puff of air and no noise at all, Lerebisa, the great owl, landed beside Mmutla. 'Greetings, little long-ears,' he said in his deep, rich voice, 'and just why are you staring up so?'

'I'm looking at the moon hare,' replied Mmutla. 'Do you know the story of his life?'

Lerebisa slowly turned his head towards Mmutla. 'I might,' he said cautiously, 'and if by any chance I did know it, what would you give me to tell it?'

'Oh, Grandfather,' said Mmutla (using a respectful word for an older person), 'you know that I, as lowly as I am, could give you nothing that would honour you sufficiently.'

Lerebisa smiled at the crude flattery and replied that, if Mmutla thought that highly of him, he would

1 a little hill.

175

tell the story for nothing. Mmutla chuckled. They both know that all Lerebisa had been looking for was attention. Lerebisa yawned, clicked his beak and moved to a more comfortable position. Then he began to tell the story.

'Long, long ago, when the gods still came down to visit the peoples of earth, the wild hare was sitting in a field and staring up at the moon, very much as you were when I found you. Suddenly, he saw a terrible sight. The great fruit bat was flying straight towards the night god's chariot. "Fruit bat, turn around, stop!" screamed the wild hare. He screamed so hard that he lost his voice. It had been a beautiful voice, clear and pure. The fruit bat heard him and swerved around, just in time to avoid a collision with the beautiful, golden chariot of the sky god.

'Thankful about the bat, but also very sad about his beautiful voice, the hare crept away. Just as he was crawling into a crack between two rocks, he felt a tap on the shoulder. "Just a minute there," he heard a deep voice say. "I saw how you saved my chariot by screaming a warning to the fruit bat. I also saw how you hurt your voice. I cannot give you back your beautiful voice, but I will promise you this: all your descendants will have a soft, scratchy voice but a voice none the less, and you I will carry with me on my journey through the sky. All on earth will remember you, little long-ears, as the one who saved the moon."'

Lerebisa stared down at Mmutla and started to see

Tshwene the baboon, Noga the python and Tau the lion all nearby, enthralled by the story. He chuckled as he rose up on his silent wings. It's amazing, he thought, how natural enemies will come together just to hear a story.

Little Brother:
The Story of an Eagle

Adam John Clulow

He clasps the crag with crooked hands;
Close to the sun with lonely lands.
Alfred Lord Tennyson

The eagles had lived in the same place for as long as anyone could remember. Hated by the farmers and and the local tribesmen, their numbers were now much diminished. These proud, noble lords had been branded 'sheep-killers' and hunted as such.

Farmer Mervyn Newmarch and his induna[1] had ploughed the lands of Whitecliff farm for thirty years. Every year they had glimpsed the great birds and sworn at them.

TRING, TRING

At last the class rose to be dismissed. The master bellowed at the retreating pupils. '*Onthou, jou vakansie projek. Iets oor voels*'.[2] Anton searched the shimmering main road for the distinctive red Nissan bakkie.[3] There it was under the old doringboom.[4] Trust Jacobus, his father's driver, to find the only shade outside the Greytown school.

As the bakkie jolted out of Greytown along the Muden road, Anton's bright-blue eyes watched the

1 head man
2 'Don't forget your holiday project. Something about birds.'
3 overland car
4 thorn tree

wide stoeped[5] settler houses flash by. The hottest day since 1956 was what his schoolmaster had told him. Anton had really enjoyed Mr Potgieter's Afrikaans and Science classes. Mr Potgieter was a fund of wildlife information. Anton knew exactly what type of bird he would study for his project: the eagle!

The gum tree marking the turn off to Whitecliff farm looked as bedraggled as ever. Anton wondered how many years it would be before it fell. As the red bakkie passed through the numerous farm gates, umfaans[6] shouted hopefully, '*Amaswidi!* Sweets.' The bakkie lurched along the rutted road through the thorn bushes, into the stone gateway, past the chicken coop, finally ending the journey at the white-washed farmhouse,

Anton hurled himself out and was met by a robust black child who came running from the chicken coop. His sweating body was covered in chicken feathers, giving him the appearance of a tarred-and-feathered cowboy from the Wild West. Without pausing to greet him Anton asked urgently, 'Are they out yet, Sibongile!'

'Yes, Inkosaan,'[7] replied Sibongile. 'The older eagle chick has hatched and now all we wait for is the small one.'

The plan which Sibongile and Anton had long

5 with wide verandas
6 young black children on the farm
7 form of address

since prepared flashed through Anton's head.

'Is the straw block ready?' he asked.

'Yes, all is ready to catch the eagle chick when he is forced out of the nest,' answered the black child proudly.

Suddenly a crack appeared in the fragile egg. A small, hesitant baby eagle's egg tooth was pushed out. Slowly the crack widened, as life expanded within the egg. A small bedraggled head followed by a fluffy white baby. The miracle of life had taken place.

The older chick stood looking on impassively. Suddenly it attacked, driven by primeval instinct to kill its sibling. The bright-yellow beak flashed like an executioner's sword, Blood spurted from the newly born chick's wound. Finally, the *coup de grâce*. The executioner pushed his victim out of the high nest, thus condemning his brother to almost certain death.

Anton woke with a start. Someone was tugging at his hair. As his eyes became accustomed to the pre-dawn light, he made out Sibongile's dark form.

'What time is it?' Anton protested sharply.

'The eagle chick, we've got him. His older brother pushed him off the nest edge right on to our straw blocks. We did it!' was the babbled reply.

'HOORAY!' screamed Anton, 'Where is he now? Is he hurt? When did you find him? I must see him now, Sibongile.'

'He is in the chicken coop, Inkosaan, waiting,'

replied Sibongile, speaking now in his usual calm voice.

The eagle chick was hidden snugly in a pile of straw. His fluffy white body was stained with dried blood. Anton carefully cradled the chick in his hands and examined him carefully. Although the chick had numerous cuts, none was deep enough to be fatal.

'He's going to live, Sibongile, he's going to live!' whispered Anton.

Anton read Mr Potgieter's notes about the diet of an eagle over and over again, until he knew them off by heart. 'Eagles require a staple diet of meat. They are therefore carnivores. The main prey of a typical eagle such as the Black Eagle, which lives on the Whitecliff hills, is the dassie. This small, brown, furry creature resembling a rabbit is found in abundance in South Africa. The baby eaglet is fed with dassie meat hunted by both the parents. The chick later learns to fend for itself. Contrary to popular belief, Black Eagles are not sheep-killers. They do, however, feed on carrion – that is, dead and decomposing animal flesh.

Anton remembered how his father cursed Black Eagles and called them sheep-killers. What if he found out about the eagle chick? His thoughts returned to the problems in hand. He could not hope to catch dassies by himself, and even with Sibongile it would be nearly impossible. Anton tried to picture an alternative to dassie meat. Chicken? No, venison? No, mince? Yes! That was it, Mince.

*

The white down was beginning to be replaced by the slightly darker adolescent feathers. The eagle, Little Brother, as they had called him, was healing slowly. Anton had decided that it was time for flying school. Early on Saturday morning, long before anyone was awake, they took Little Brother to the Bushman's rock. This was so named because legend says it was on this very rock that Bushman hunters watched for game.

Little Brother was perched on a branch held between Sibongile and Anton. As they climbed the final hill, Bushman's rock came into sight.

'There it is,' shouted Anton. 'There's where you learn to fly, Little Brother.'

The rock itself was easy to climb because of the numerous cracks for feet and hands. As they reached the top, the full strength of the icy early morning wind struck them. Anton started flapping his arms, trying to demonstrate the flapping motion of a parent Black Eagle.

'Like this, Little Brother, like this,' urged Anton.

Little Brother watched Anton without moving. The longer Anton flapped, the more uninterested the bird became.

'Come on, Sibongile. He's not even interested. Let's go,' said Anton.

'Hup, one, two, three, four. Hup, one, two, three. Hup . . .' They marched homewards. Suddenly Anton's father appeared.

'What's all the row,' he exclaimed. Then he stopped dead in his tracks as he saw Little Brother.

ENTRIES FROM THE EAGLE PROJECT BY
ANTON NEWMARCH

Monday, 9 July

Today we attempted to get Little Brother to fly. We were not successful and therefore decided to return to the 'drawing board'. On the way home we were intercepted by my father. He was angry that we had taken an eagle chick under our care. Eventually, with the aid of Mr Potgieter's notes, we managed to persuade father that eagles are not sheep-killers. He agreed to help us raise Little Brother.

My father shot a pair of dassies near the river. As a special present to Little Brother, Dad cut up the meat into slivers and fed the eagle. Little Brother gorged himself hungrily, eating a whole dassie. We have decided that we are again going to try to get Little Brother to fly.

Tuesday, 17 July

Today Little Brother learned to fly thanks to my father. We threw slivers of dassie meat on the ground below the foot of Bushman's rock. We then took Little Brother to the peak of the rock so that he had to fly to reach the meat. As we increased the distance between the meat and our eagle, Little Brother flew for the first time. We were very proud of him!

Wednesday, 25 July

Today Little Brother took his first bath. We woke early to find puddles everywhere. It had rained

186

heavily for the first time in months and the deep tyre tracks of our bakkie were overflowing with water. Little Brother peered fascinated into the puddles. With a tentative claw he probed the water. Suddenly, with a loud squawk, Little Brother lost his balance and tippled into the puddle. He screeched, he flapped, he dipped his head and then proceeded to paddle up along the river of ruts.

Thereafter Little Brother took a daily bath in our old washing tub, which we filled with tepid water.

Saturday, 4 August

The next landmark in Little Brother's life was his first kill, which was essential to his survival if he was to be released into the wild. For weeks we had been throwing dassie meat to Little Brother as his daily meal. But today we had decided to make him fight for his meal by tying the dassie to a piece of thick string. As Little Brother advanced towards his meat, we jerked it out of his beak's reach. Annoyed, he hopped forward. Another jerk. Angry now, Little Brother flew to the meat. Another pull on the string. With outstretched claws Little Brother landed directly on the meat. He had learned to chase.

Little Brother's hunting lessons became quickly more advanced until his first kill. Little Brother's first kill was an animal of the deadly species, the gecko. He swooped down on the small lizard as if he had been hunting all his life.

His first dassie was a baby unluckily separated

from its mother. Little Brother saw his opportunity and dropped down, fierce claws outstretched. A few minutes later he returned to a rocky ledge to enjoy his meal.

Monday, 1 October
Tomorrow I must say goodbye to Little Brother for the last time. It has been decided that it is time that Little Brother be released back into the wild. With the help of father we have persuaded the Parks Board at Epongeni Game Reserve. I will never forget him and the adventures we had.

The tears were streaming freely down Anton's face.

'Farewell, Little Brother. You will always be in my heart. Goodbye, goodbye,' wept Anton. The majestic eagle rose, circled once over the hutted Epongeni camp and slowly glided off into the azure sky.

A Race Against Time

Sheya Shipanga

It was a dark, cold and foggy evening. Melanie was standing at her windowsill. It was an eerie night and the streets were deserted. A single ray of light was shining from the streetlamp opposite her house. Then she noticed a long, sprawly shadow. Her heart jumped a beat. Someone was there. It was not a familiar figure; it was an old man, dressed in Victorian clothing. He had a long, black coat around his shoulders, which was turned up at the collar. On his head was a black top hat. Melanie could not see his face, because it was turned towards the sky. Who or what was he?

Melanie was afraid. She wanted to scream. It must be a ghost, or was it her own imagination playing tricks on her? Quickly she drew the curtains together.

'Are you all right, Melanie?'

It was her mother.

'I'm fine, Mum. I didn't hear you come in,' Melanie replied.

'I came to say goodnight. It's getting late.'

Melanie said goodnight to her mother, and then she was left alone again.

Melanie was nervous. Was he still there? She decided to be courageous and take another look out of the window. Thank goodness, he had vanished.

She must have been imagining. She climbed into bed, ready to switch off her lamp. The rest of the house was in darkness. It was a large, old house, which had been lived in for many years by her father's family. Just as she was about to switch off her lamp, she heard a voice. Someone was calling her.

'Melanie! Melanie!'

She swung around to look behind her. There stood the stranger in Victorian clothing.

'Don't be afraid,' he said. 'I only want to talk to you.'

Melanie, all of a sudden, felt a shiver run up her spine.

'H-how do you know my name? What do you want?' she cried.

'I need your help, Melanie. You see, I'm your great-great-grandfather.'

Could it be true? She looked at his face. It was wrinkled and weatherbeaten.

'Then you would be a ghost,' exclaimed Melanie.

'I'm not a ghost. Here, feel my hands.'

He was walking towards her, bringing the fusty stench of hundreds of years with him.

She was too scared to refuse. He was now standing opposite her. She slowly stretched out her hand and touched his. It was icy cold, and bony, but perfectly solid.

'I am your great-great-grandfather, but not a ghost. Only time could really explain that to you. The world may soon go corrupt, unless you can help.'

'How? Why?' she asked.

'Soon people from the past, present and future will all be living in one era. Can you imagine what the world will be like? Some evil force is pulling people from the past and future into your era. We do not want to do this, but we are given no choice.'

'You mean that you are one of these people?' Melanie asked.

'Yes. I am the first one. There is a way that you can help, if you are willing.'

Melanie did not know what to say. It was all too confusing.

'Tell me what I must do,' she finally answered.

'If you can destroy something that once belonged to me, you can prevent me from entering your era. If I cannot enter, nobody else can. The hardest task is to find something easy enough to destroy. Although, you have only until sunrise tomorrow. As soon as the sun comes up, the second person will enter, then the next . . .'

'Where do I look?' she asked. But it was too late. He had disappeared into thin air.

Melanie wanted to hide under her covers and fall asleep, but she knew that she could not ignore reality. The world was counting on her. She climbed out of bed and put on her nightgown. Whatever she did, she had to be quiet. Where should she look? What if there was nothing within the house that belonged to him? She did not even know his name. He could only be from her father's side of the family, because her mother was French.

She would just have to try her best. She took a candle from her drawer and lit it. She switched off her bedroom light and left the room. She knew the house perfectly well, but some rooms were locked. The playroom was next to her room, so she went there first. There was nothing of interest, except for an old doll's house. It was hopeless. Then she remembered the attic. That was a good place to look for old things. Silently, she made her way. The house was still and spooky. She climbed the stairs on to the top floor. The attic door was unlocked, so she managed to get inside. It was a dusty, smelly attic. In one corner was a pile of books, and in another corner some old clothes. She looked at the clothes. They were impossible to distinguish. She studied the room. On the ceiling was a trapdoor, which she had never noticed before.

She pulled up a small, wooden chair. By standing on the chair, she could just manage to reach the little trapdoor. She pushed open the flap, and put the candle on to the floor. It was now easier to lift herself up. It was a tiny room. There was a cardboard box, and a wooden chest by the wall. The chest was locked, but beside it lay a large sheet of paper. She spread it out on to the floor. It was a family tree. The first thing she noticed was her great-great-grandfather's name: Robert Clayton. It was a start, she supposed. Melanie opened the cardboard box. It was full of ornaments. Something caught her eye. It was the handle of an old, black walking-stick. She took it out of the box. There was an inscription on the side. Two letters, R. and C. Could they be initials? If so, did they belong to her great-great-grandfather? It was old enough.

She scrambled through the box. There was nothing else. She had to take a chance. Time was running out. Walking-stick in one hand, candle in the other, she went back to the flap. Dropping the stick down first, she climbed carefully down with the candle. She them picked up the walking-stick and crept out of the attic. She decided that she would burn the walking-stick. Next to the kitchen was an old stove which nobody used. Melanie made her way down to the kitchen. There stood the stove. She gave the handle a jerk. It swung open. Inside was a heap of unused coal. In the kitchen she found a box of matches. She came back and lit the stove. It was soon burning strongly. She took one more look at the walking-stick and then put it in the stove to burn.

It was getting late, well past midnight. If the walking-stick did not burn by sunrise, there would be no more hope. What if the walking-stick did not even belong to her great-great-grandfather? She shoved more coal on to the fire and went back up to bed. The whole night she could not sleep. When sunrise finally came, she jumped out of bed and rushed down to the kitchen. Her heart was beating fast. Had she dreamt everything? Quickly, she opened the stove door. There was a big pile of ashes. The walking-stick had burnt to nothing. Suddenly she had the feeling that someone was watching her. She turned around. There was the figure.

'You did well, Melanie. Well . . .'

Melanie wanted to speak, but he had faded away. That was the last time that she would see him.

Her mother came into the kitchen.

'What's wrong, Melanie? What are you doing?'

'I'm sorry I frightened you, Mum. I had a bad dream,' she replied.

It had been like a nightmare, but it was no dream.

'Come along. You'll feel better after breakfast,' her mother said. 'What was the dream about?'

'A race, and I won.'